T0318708

Cambridge Elements ≡

Elements in Psychology and Culture
edited by
Kenneth D. Keith
University of San Diego

CHILD HELPERS

A Multidisciplinary Perspective

David F. Lancy

Utah State University

CAMBRIDGE
UNIVERSITY PRESS

CAMBRIDGE
UNIVERSITY PRESS

University Printing House, Cambridge CB2 8BS, United Kingdom

One Liberty Plaza, 20th Floor, New York, NY 10006, USA

477 Williamstown Road, Port Melbourne, VIC 3207, Australia

314–321, 3rd Floor, Plot 3, Splendor Forum, Jasola District Centre,
New Delhi – 110025, India

79 Anson Road, #06–04/06, Singapore 079906

Cambridge University Press is part of the University of Cambridge.

It furthers the University's mission by disseminating knowledge in the pursuit of
education, learning, and research at the highest international levels of excellence.

www.cambridge.org
Information on this title: www.cambridge.org/9781108738552
DOI: 10.1017/9781108769204

First published 2020

A catalogue record for this publication is available from the British Library.

ISBN 978-1-108-73855-2 Paperback
ISSN 2515-3986 (online)
ISSN 2515-3943 (print)

Child Helpers

A Multidisciplinary Perspective

Elements in Psychology and Culture

DOI: 10.1017/9781108769204
First published online: February 2020

David F. Lancy
Utah State University

Author for correspondence: David F. Lancy, david.lancy@usu.edu

Abstract: In most of the worlds' distinct cultures, children – from toddlerhood – eagerly volunteer to help others with their chores. Laboratory research in child psychology supports the claim that the helper "stage" is biologically based. This Element examines the development of helping in varied cultural contexts, in particular, reviewing evidence for supportive environments in the ethnographic record versus an environment that extinguishes the drive to be helpful in WEIRD children. In the last section, the benefits of the helper stage are discussed, specifically the development of an ability to work and learn collaboratively.

Keywords: child, helper, developmental stage, ethnographic studies, lab experiments

ISBNs: 9781108738552 (PB), 9781108769204 (OC)
ISSNs: 2515-3986 (online), 2515-3943 (print)

Contents

1 Juvenile Helpers

1.1 Overview

This Element was greatly inspired by a 15-minute film titled *Tiny Katerina*, which shows glimpses of Katerina from two- to four-and-a-half years of age. She lives with her parents and older brother in Northwestern Siberia in the taiga. The Khanty-speaking people live by foraging (berries, for example), fishing, and herding reindeer; they are seminomadic. Their camp and its surrounding vicinity show no evidence of electricity or any other public service. These people are very much "off the grid." From the first, as a wobbly toddler, Katerina is shown being helpful. She carries (and drops and picks up) firewood chopped by her mother into their tent. She ladles food (spilling some) from a large pot over the fire into a tin and feeds the dog. She carries pans with bread dough to her mother to place in the baking oven. When her mother goes gathering in the forest, Katerina has her own toddler-size collecting bucket. She is out in all weather, including deep snow, keeping warm in her animal skin anorak and mittens.

Katerina and her mother treat her myriad helping activities – imitating and collaborating with her mother – as absolutely routine (Golovnev, 2004; Golovnev & Golovneva, 2016). In a visceral way, the film reveals the deep gulf between our *Western, Educated, Industrialized, Rich, Democracy* (WEIRD) (Henrich, Heine, & Norenzayan, 2010; Kline, Shamsudheen, & Broesch, 2018) model of "normal" child development and child-rearing and the view derived from the anthropology of childhood.

As often noted, human life history is unique in encompassing an extremely long (by mammalian and, especially, primate standards) period of juvenility. Bogin (2006: 205) claims that recognizable and unique stages are *added* to the primate life course: child, juvenile (I use "middle childhood"), and adolescent. Many theories account for this extraordinary pattern, such as that children are slowly acquiring "embodied capital" in terms of physical size, strength, immunities, survival tactics, and facility with social relationships (Kaplan & Bock, 2001). But all perspectives emphasize that juveniles are in a state of dependency, unable to meet their own needs – they are "costly." This costly and prolonged investment in one's offspring is quite evident in WEIRD society. In fact, even as the birthrate has declined dramatically, the amount of time, effort, and money that WEIRD parents expend on child-rearing has increased substantially (Doepke & Filibotti, 2019). Not only is the investment quite high but also returns, at least as far as children "paying back" by contributing to the domestic economy, are scanty – at least since the 1960s (Goodnow, 1988) or earlier: "The advice literature of the 1920s through the 1940s often sought . . . to encourage the [growth] of the democratically organized family, [where

Figure 1.1 – Katerina (Russia: Ivan Golovnev)

children] would be *psychologically* incorporated into their families as equals, rather than earn that role through their economic contributions" (Fass, 2016: 107). In fact, in WEIRD society most children's "work," such as homework or practicing the piano, is strictly for the benefit of the child and may impose an added burden on parents, who help with homework and pay for piano lessons. But the WEIRD pattern is anomalous and characterized as "one of the worst subpopulations one could study for generalizing about *Homo sapiens*" (Henrich et al., 2010: 79). A critical mass of research in traditional societies has accumulated that uncovers children's ability and inclination to, at least partially, "pay back" their benefactors (Kramer, 2011). Discounting WEIRD society – where children are viewed as carefree, playful "cherubs" – as an outlier, we should reconsider and see children as helpful and hardworking would-be citizens, like Katerina.

Work maps onto nearly the entire juvenile period, and it is entwined with developmental processes. The juvenile's physical abilities, understanding of the environment, technical skill, strength, endurance, and assumption of responsibility all show clear developmental trends that are applied to or activated by participation in the activities of older role models or through the individual conduct of routine chores (Lancy 2018). It is important to stress that – outside WEIRD society – while infants and toddlers may be indulged, having all their needs met and enjoying nearly unlimited playtime, sooner or later they will be expected to shoulder a share of the domestic routine. How much they work and how soon varies cross-culturally, but it is the trajectory that all will eventually follow.

The helper "stage," which begins as early as fourteen months and lasts several years, is preparatory for a life of collaborative, family/community–based work. As one measure of the centrality of work in the child's development, we find several societies that apply distinctive terms to characterize each stage. For example,

> In the Giriama (Kenya) language the term for a child roughly two through three years in age is *kahoho kuhuma madzi*: a youngster who can be sent to fetch a cup of water. ... A girl, from about eight years until approximately puberty, is *muhoho wa kubunda*, a child who pounds maize; a boy of this age is a *muhoho murisa*, a child who herds. (Wenger, 1989: 98)

The *helper* stage entails several distinctive characteristics, including that the child's desire to help may outpace their ability to be useful, at least in the endeavor they have offered to contribute to. Adults and older siblings must, therefore, manage the young helper. Even the youngest helpers may be seen as having unique attributes that make them ideal for certain jobs, such as gossip courier. So, not all work during the helper stage is strictly "developmental."

The very young suffer from quite low status, and voluntary helping is often a key that admits the child to limited participation, which, in turn, raises their social standing. Families may encourage the would-be helper by donating scaled-down or discarded tools for practice. Or, as an example of crafts, a potter may give her little girl a ball of clay to play with and then take her crude results and reform them into recognizable miniature pots. With few exceptions, indigenous communities act as if they fully expect children to volunteer to help out and, unlike WEIRD society (Pettygrove et al., 2013; Dahl et al., 2017), see no need to explicitly encourage, teach, reward, praise, or thank the child for being helpful.[1]

---

[1] The literature is littered with various terms to designate the sorts of small-scale, face-to-face communities historically documented by anthropologists. Among these terms, which I will use somewhat interchangeably, are "indigenous," "heritage," and "traditional." I find "village" the most congenial and expressive of the contrast with WEIRD society.

The helper stage can also be viewed as a *developmental niche* (Super & Harkness, 1986). The construct describes a system with a confluence of everyday practices (*habitus*, cf. Bourdieu, 1977), parenting *ethnotheory* (Harkness et al., 2010) and practice, and the child's biological growth and development. More specifically, the facilitating behavior of parents and others as workers, such as acting as willing role models to be observed and imitated, the ready availability of tools to practice with, and the plethora of sub-tasks in any undertaking all contribute to an environment that is adapted to the nurturance of eager but clumsy helpers. Elsewhere, I have characterized this interactive program to promote children's development as workers as the "chore curriculum" (Lancy, 2012).

Section 2 discusses three aspects of the infant's early experience prior to the onset of the helper stage. While all young children seem to share a need to be helpful, culturally rooted motives are plentiful. Setting aside the extreme indulgence granted infants in a few foraging societies, most infants and toddlers are subtly reminded of their debt to those who feed and care for them. "Delayed personhood" is an extremely common notion in which the acknowledgment that one is worthy of full membership in the community and the conferral of a "real" name and identity are deferred. In a systematic survey of thirty-two foraging societies, bands or communities were composed, primarily, of unrelated individuals, suggesting that membership is not an automatic right conferred by kinship but must be earned through cooperative, prosocial behavior (Hill et al., 2011). Drawing on several complementary theories from psychology, a case is made that this culturally constructed sense of obligation reinforces the biological imperative to help.

While the socialization of helpers may be quite subtle and nondirective, that is not always true of a complementary virtue: sharing. In small-scale, face-to-face societies – especially those that rely on the uncertain availability of wild foods – a willingness to share is the *sine qua non* of social life. The propensity to share may be what makes us unique as a species, compared to chimpanzees, for example (Hrdy, 2009). The sharing and transfer of food and other valued resources range from the commonplace – feeding the very young and the elderly – to the colorful and ceremonious such as the Trobriand Islands *Kula* or the PNG Highlands' "sing sing"(Barnett, 1938; Mauss, 1967). Apparently, children do not offer to share a treasured snack or other prize as readily as they offer to help. Hence, many societies embrace an explicit program of training the very young to be unselfish. The willingness to share, especially products the child has acquired through their own gathering or hunting, is as highly esteemed as volunteer helping. As noted in this subsection, helping may look somewhat different depending on the nature of work. While gardening, for example, is typically done collaboratively, gathering or hunting in the forest is typically executed by individuals, even while foraging in groups. Even very young children may find themselves in possession of valued resources, such as baobab fruits they have gathered under the trees. They "help" by sharing the results of these labors.

Helping is also facilitated via an entirely different source – the imperative to engage in make-believe or mimicry. Play is nearly universal in early childhood, and surveys of the ethnographic record note that make-believe or play that replicates the patterns of behavior on view in the child's family and wider community occupies a significant portion of "playtime." Unlike make-believe play in WEIRD society, the "scripts" are drawn from reality, particularly scenes of older members at work. While play and work are juxtaposed as antithetical in WEIRD society, elsewhere play is seen as complementary to the work children do or aspire to do. The very young (and their older caretakers) are very inventive when it comes to replicating scenes from daily life – using materials and objects readily at hand. Hence, a little girl's doll will be carried, coddled, fed, and cleaned in make-believe play before the girl steps into the role of alloparent, ditto for cooking, food preparation, crafts (such as weaving), herding (using clay animals), hoeing, chopping, hut building, and so on. The great value of play is that it allows the child to advance along the trajectory toward "being useful" without harming valued commodities or the children themselves, and it also avoids the need to interrupt or question an adult to solicit tuition.

In Section 3, we look at the helper stage through the lenses of anthropology and psychology. The evidence reviewed for anthropology emphasizes the wide range of societies and situations where child helpers or wannabe helpers have been observed. Particular attention is paid to ethnographic accounts that reveal the great enthusiasm the very young invest in their desires and efforts to be helpful. In developmental psychology, interest in child helpers has been minimal until quite recently. Led by Felix Warneken and Michael Tomasello, a growing series of studies has simulated situations where children as young as fourteen months are afforded an opportunity to be helpful. With each new study, the robustness and reliability of what appears to be a heritable drive to assist is affirmed and broadened. The notion that the child's drive to be helpful is finite in duration – a stage or critical period – is easier to construct from the ethnographic data than from the lab studies. The samples used in these studies to date have not been older than about age three-and-a-half.

Research reviewed in Section 3 makes a strong case that the helper stage is universal. Indeed, almost all the lab studies have used WEIRD children as subjects; so, we must assume that WEIRD toddlers are as desirous of "pitching in" as their village counterparts. Yet, while the village kids are solid citizens by middle childhood, contributing in myriad ways to the domestic economy, WEIRD kids of the same age are reluctant participants who are more likely to resist entreaties than to volunteer.[2] The cause, as argued in Section 4, is the failure to accept and welcome toddlers' helping overtures, which leads to the extinction of the drive to be helpful.

Notwithstanding the early, spontaneous emergence of helping during the helper stage, older children offer varying levels of support for their family and peers. This may range from near zero in at least two societies of note – WEIRD and the Dobe !Kung (Draper, 1976) – to providing vital services (herding, infant care, food preparation) and resources (harvested crops, gathered tubers and fruits) on a consistent, reliable basis. Helpers transition smoothly into self-guided, self-sufficient *workers*. How this variation comes about is the subject of Section 4. The resolution lies in the degree of accommodation that the family and community make during the helper stage and after to children who are eager to participate and learn on the job. For example, in an indigenous Kichwa (Ecuadorian Andes) community, mothers were more effective at supporting the child's spontaneous efforts to be helpful than were WEIRD mothers from Münster, Germany. As a result, "indigenous children helped more often, helped in a more spontaneous way, and helped in more complex and risky tasks (implying more skillful participation) than Münster children" (Giner Torréns, Coppens, & Kärtner, 2019).

The ethnographic record is replete with descriptions of child helpers being woven into the fabric of daily life, including the full panoply of domestic work – from fetching firewood to butchering game to making tortillas. The would-be helper is not given *carte blanche*, but even the most inept toddler is assigned a task that is within their capacity, and there is great tolerance for the child's experimentation with the "tools of the trade," including sharp knives. While child helpers are not lavishly praised or rewarded, milestones of new chores completed or tasks mastered (first animal kill) are celebrated.

Section 4.2 reviews evidence from WEIRD culture for the extinction of the drive to be helpful. Although this research is by no means voluminous, several sources indicate a lack of enthusiasm for infant helpers. Would-be beneficiaries find that allowing children to pitch in makes the task more difficult and slows

---

[2] As I was writing this paragraph, my daughter – mother of a new baby – sent me the following from a Facebook post. A blogging Mom writes "Y'all . . . I am in total shock. Like push me over with a feather. My 6 year old has a friend over and they were arguing about what to do next. I jokingly said, 'What if you two clean the whole house?' They looked at each other. The friend said 'That's a great idea.' My son said 'Let's do it.' They are cleaning. Right. Now." Those who commented on this post shared her amazement.

down the process. Rather than allowing would-be helpers to become involved in, for example, meal preparation or gardening, the WEIRD parent may refocus the task at hand so that it becomes a lesson in nutrition or botany.

These two broad patterns of incorporating helpful children into the domestic economy versus spurning or trying to postpone the helpful child's debut have different end points. In traditional societies, the desire to be helpful is carefully nurtured. Predictably, these children mature into vital contributors to the welfare of their family and community. For these children, as the helper stage ends, the *worker* stage begins. Children in WEIRD society, by contrast, thwarted in their desire to pitch in, seem to readily adapt to a lifestyle where they are wholly the beneficiaries of others' good works, with little or no obligation to reciprocate. They become excellent candidates for the "failure to launch" syndrome (Lancy, 2017a).

Section 4.3 speculates on the end of the helper stage. The end point may fall earlier or later, depending on the demand for the child's labor, but it is broadly encompassed by the period of middle childhood, roughly ages six to ten. During this period, a variety of subtle changes will occur in the child's involvement in the domestic economy. They will act more independently in reliably completing chores, and these will be more demanding in terms of strength and skill than chores taken on earlier. Children will have become more competent as gatherers or hunters and are able to make a significant contribution to their own and the family's diet. In WEIRD society, the child-worker role is eclipsed by the role of student. Increasing numbers of WEIRD children are expected to become strivers academically, athletically, socially, and artistically. They may be every bit as hard working as their village counterparts but just not very helpful.

Throughout this Element, I try to keep the question of benefits in view. These are not only not obvious but can even be counterintuitive. Why should playful children without responsibility *volunteer* to work? Why should the targets of potentially meddlesome helpers tolerate them? Section 5 provides two significant responses. First, the very basis of humanity is argued to be our capacity for collaboration. When toddlers seek to pitch in, they are making a bid to collaborate. Unlike the lab paradigm, where the help is aimed at a specific act (picking up a lost item) for a specific person with a specific need, in the village setting the helper has a more complex agenda. As Hrdy's (2016) analysis shows, acting effectively as a collaborator is extremely challenging and completely beyond the ability of nonhuman primates. The helper stage sets up the "classroom" to nurture the skills essential to effective collaboration. A second benefit of the commitment to being helpful identified in Section 5 is the practice and development of social learning skills, such as learning through attending to others' speech (over hearing). Once helpers have been taken on board the team, so to speak, they will be able to closely observe others who are competent; imitate what they have seen;

and judge, from the way their work is received, whether their performance is adequate.

1.2 Reconsidering Juvenile Dependency

One of the cornerstones of human life history is the recognition of a uniquely extended period of juvenility (Bogin, 2006). Aside from delayed reproduction, juvenility, in most theories, is defined by juveniles remaining largely dependent on others for most of their needs for up to two decades. As there is little consensus on how to stage childhood or how to name the stages (Grove & Lancy, 2015), in this Element, I use "juvenile" to describe the entire period of dependency, or the period when the individual is at least somewhat dependent on others for provisioning, shelter, and so on.[3] The juvenile is, effectively, *subsidized* (Kramer & Greaves, 2011). Of course, the period of greatest dependency is infancy, followed by childhood or early childhood, from ages two to six. Next comes middle childhood, from ages seven to ten, followed by adolescence. The age ranges are approximate. In societies where the domestic economy requires high labor inputs from family members, children may move on to the next stage more quickly. While helping is characteristic of the entire juvenile period except early infancy, I argue that the helper stage is associated with late infancy and early childhood, ending in middle childhood.

The extended juvenile period in humans, relative to other mammals, is a costly reproductive strategy in terms of the need for prolonged parental investment coupled with the risk that one's offspring will expire before reaching reproductive potential. One solution to this quandary is for juveniles to help out, leading to a "bidirectional transfer of resources and labor between juveniles, mothers and others" (Kramer, 2011: 535). However, seeing human juveniles as making a significant contribution to the pooled labor of the family has only been acknowledged and documented relatively recently. Among indigenous people, of course, it is taken for granted and unremarkable:

> When Maya children from the Yucatan Peninsula were asked why they helped, they seemed surprised by the question; the answer seemed obvious to them. One child responded, "I help because I live there," and another mentioned, "Helping is everybody's responsibility." (Rogoff et al., 2017: 881)
> Among the Tikopia (Melanesia), the ideal child seeks social participation and interdependence ... the motivation to work ... lay in the situation itself

---

[3] As a small caveat, I would note that elderly women have been referred to as helpers because their work is now directed at the support of their extended kin rather than their own nuclear family (Blurton Jones, Hawkes, & O'Connell, 2005), and they are also dependent on others for at least some of their basic needs. These helpers lie outside the scope of this Element.

with the worker embedded in society and thereby gaining social value. (Lee, 1961: 29)

There are several reasons for earlier views that saw the juvenile period as a unidirectional transfer of resources from adult to child. First, the Harvard studies of the Dobe !Kung of the Kalahari (Botswana) offered one of the earliest and most comprehensive studies of hunter-gatherer (H-G) childhood and concluded that !Kung "children do amazingly little work" (Draper, 1976: 213). Research with other H-G societies and, indeed, further studies of the !Kung as well suggest that this statement cannot be widely generalized. H-G juveniles vary in their contributions, but some degree of involvement in the domestic economy appears to be universal.

Another early idea was that humans required an extended period of subsidized or "sheltered learning" to master the myriad and complex skills and beliefs that would allow them to fulfill their role as adult members of the community. Children were seen as learners, unable to apply their nascent skills until they and their skills had more fully matured – much the way WEIRD children apply school learning only years later in work. Village technology (with rare exceptions such as that of the Inuit), however, tends to be quite simple and transparent. Kramer's research demonstrates that children's skill level is driven by the time logged exercising the skill, which suggests that children "learn by doing" (Kramer & Greaves, 2011; Kramer, 2019; see also Koster, Bruno, & Burns, 2016). Even with the most rudimentary skill and understanding of how to use a bow and arrows, a mortar and pestle, a sharp knife, or a digging stick, juveniles can supplement or support the efforts of others (Blurton Jones, & Marlowe, 2002).

The Hadza (Tanzania; Crittenden et al., 2013), Mer Islanders (Melanesia; Bird & Bird, 2002), and the Mikea (Madagascar; Tucker & Young, 2005) are three well-documented cases of societies where young children master their environments to the extent of being able to acquire wild edible resources, such as small mammals, birds, shellfish, and wild tubers. Successful child foragers not only supplement their own diet but also share their catch with others, particularly younger siblings, consuming it on the spot or carrying it back to camp to share with the family. Sharing "food may act to build and maintain social bonds" (Crittenden, 2016a: 64).

But even these very thorough studies do not convey the complete picture. In addition to food acquisition, children strive to reduce their burden on their seniors by performing various domestic services, such as fetching firewood; caring for younger siblings; and assisting with food processing, cooking, and so on. Far from seeing children as costly dependents burdening their caretakers for years, Kramer asserts, "Children's help . . . minimizes demands on parental care and maximizes maternal time and energy available for reproduction and infant care" (Kramer, 2011: 537; see also Stanton et al., 2017). Taking it further, I found clear evidence that juveniles can quickly ratchet up their contributions to family and community in response to times of critical need, such as the death of relatives and periods of food scarcity, warfare, and plague (Lancy, 2015a). Children pitching in to help or taking the initiative to learn useful skills on their own are the earliest signs of a precocious effort to lessen dependency on others and to act (and be treated) like a contributing member of the group. It is just possible, however, that focusing on dependency as *the* attribute of the juvenile period has led to a failure to appreciate the young child's critical role as helper.

1.3 The Helper Stage in Child Development

The idea that juveniles should be viewed as helpful to others (taking care of baby brother while mother works, sharing food they have collected) pervades this analysis. Here, however, I want to introduce a central issue, namely helping during a period that I label the "helper stage." This stage in a child's development spans fourteen months of age to, approximately, seven years or middle childhood. In Section 3, I discuss research from anthropology and psychology aimed at demarcating the onset of the stage and detailing some of the characteristics of the helper in late infancy/early childhood. In Section 4, I discuss the end of the helper stage. Taken together, this research suggests that the helper stage encompasses a critical period where the would-be helper must be made welcome, else the helping motive is extinguished. Cross-culturally, this termination of the desire to be helpful is rare but appears to be a growing phenomenon among WEIRD families with juveniles.

The lab research on child helpers now being carried out with WEIRD samples (to be discussed later) obviously requires a brief, concise operational definition of the behavior of interest: "Helping is here defined as an action that primarily serves to facilitate the acquisition of another person's goal" (Dahl, 2015: 1080). But an anthropological lens reveals many facets to the phenomenon. This is a sampling of inferences I have drawn from fieldwork and published accounts of children helping. Obviously, the helper stage emerges at a very early age – in late infancy, in fact. Margaret Mead observed on Samoa: "The *tiniest little staggerer* has tasks to perform – to carry water, to borrow fire brands, to fetch leaves to stuff the pig" (Mead, 1928: 633, italics added). Mead's observations would find many parallels in the notes of field anthropologists (see Table 3.1).

Children who have moved into the helper stage are usually volunteers. These young would-be workers are, in effect, on probation. There is a clear risk of

Figure 1.2 – Jug Carrier (Laos: David F. Lancy)

doing more harm than good or offering help that is actually unhelpful (Wynn, 2009). Among the !Kung, "children can be a hindrance to the work groups of men and women" (Draper, 1976: 210), but they are given great latitude to learn and figure things out on their own.

A prominent characteristic of domestic chores is that they tend to get pragmatically sorted into tasks of varying difficulty (Lancy, 2018). With the guidance of someone older, who can match their capabilities to the task inventory, young children can meet their aspiration to help. The very young might volunteer to join a firewood-gathering party. Perhaps they can assist in the gathering of hay for fodder. Being asked to run an errand (borrowing a fire brand) represents a kind of "promotion" at this early stage in the development of the individual's "career" as a worker.

Aside from errands, some jobs seem particularly suited to young children. In pastoralist Kurdish (Iraq) society, from the time children are able to balance a tea glass and saucer in the one hand across the floor, they must distribute the items for the tea ritual: "The woman who makes the tea has nothing to do with serving it, and never moves from her position behind the samovar . . . as a rule it is children's work" (Hansen, 1961: 49). Children are also designated as gossip couriers:

> In Ese Eja communities (Bolivian Amazon), children . . . walk in and out of households as they wish and, since they are not cordoned off from much of adult life, they occupy a unique position to collect and traffic information. . . . In fact, adults often encourage children to gather sensitive information about others such as . . . who is having an affair with whom. . . . Children, like drunks, are not held responsible for what they say and are thus able to vocalize sensitive issues and conflicts otherwise indiscreet for adults. (Peluso, 2015: 54)

The child helper is an intern, a novice or in training. They help because they cannot yet do the tasks being carried out by the fully competent, but they are learning through participating. To borrow a phrase, helpers are "learning through observing and pitching in" (LOPI) (Paradise & Rogoff, 2009). Among the Baka (Cameroon), novice helpers were observed participating in butchering; gathering forest products, such as mushrooms and insects; and weir fishing. These tasks were subtly restructured to accommodate the child's limitations (Sonoda, 2016).

"Helper" also signals the ephemeral nature of the services that very young children provide, such as stirring the stewpot. It is not the magnitude, finesse, or urgency of the task that matters, but that the young child contributes to a legitimate or authentic component of domestic activity (Lave & Wenger, 1991). In this process, the helper may well be moving into a chore normally undertaken by an older child. There are many opportunities for advancement.

Because young children tend to be volunteers, their contribution earns social capital; their social standing rises:

> A [Nahua, Mexico] child who willingly helps and participates alongside the group is understood to be creating reciprocal relationships with others around him. For this reason, the child is understood to be "respectful." . . . *Respeto*, furthermore, implies that the individual has been converted into a person – into a fully mature human being who has earned the status of community member. (Flores et al., 2015: 328–9)

Children have opportunities to earn social capital through "good deeds." If these good deeds are voluntary and not assigned, so much the better. Florence Weiss describes this phenomenon in the Iatmul culture (Sepik Region, PNG). Children are expected to contribute to the family's efforts but are not assigned chores. Rather, their autonomy enables them to aid others and, hence, to establish lasting and valuable relationships, as when a six-year-old girl gives her aunt some of the fruit she has collected. The aunt will not only be pleased but can be counted on "to support the girl in any future need she may have" (Weiss, 1993: 119, translated in Leibel, 2004: 83). Among the Iñupiaq (Canadian Arctic), children provide critical support to the family through their labor. A young informant explains: "They respect[ed] me, because I could do ... my chores ... without them telling me. That's my reward [but sometimes] I got reward[ed] with good meals" (Sprott, 2002: 229).

Volunteering also means they are not held to the same standards of account-ability, competence, and dependability as children who have graduated from this stage. Alternatively, no one complains if they remain at the periphery observing. Indeed, for the very young, evidence that they are observing and listening attentively is as likely to earn acknowledgment as volunteering to help. Fundamentally, the child who is engaged directly or passively with the work of others is demonstrating good sense, good manners, and good morals:

> Mexicans define being *acomedido/a* as helping not because one has been asked to but because one acts on an opportunity to pitch in. Such collaborative interactions are characterized by ready helping (López et al., 2012: 876, [but] one does not want to be a nuisance when helping because of not knowing what is going on [which] highlights the importance of keenly observing ongoing activities and knowing when and how to pitch in. (López et al., 2012: 879)

A helper's offer to assist may be rebuffed or declined if they might seriously disrupt the work at hand. There is then a period when children are not yet ready to be granted the status of helper (Medaets, 2016; Michelet, 2016). In most societies, these unhelpful helpers are urged to observe, listen, and pay attention. They may be given scaled-down or old tools or a doll to use in playful practice. Samoan "children begin to practice tasks before they are expected to be capable of doing them. Toddlers try to sweep up leaves, cut the grass with a machete, or peel vegetables and are usually allowed to handle the tools required for such tasks" (Ochs, 1988: 160).

A recent study among Hadza and BaYaka foragers found that children are, generally, welcome to join foraging parties as valued helpers as well as to facilitate learning. However, there were various grounds to veto their participa-tion such as the anticipated distance or their inability to quietly stalk when prey was spotted. Or the child might be left behind due to "concerns regarding dangers included weather ... presence of elephants, lack of food, having to walk through deep waters, or risks involving climbing on rocks" (Lew-Levy et al., 2019: 313). In another peripheral role, the very young aspirant may shadow or apprentice to an older sibling who has earned acceptance as a helper.

To sum up this portrait of the helper stage: rural, small-scale societies seem to offer a *developmental niche* (Super & Harkness, 1986) in which the child's emerging prosocial tendencies (as contrasted with countervailing selfish and antisocial tendencies!) can blossom.[4]

The helping stage eventually gives way to the worker stage, but many aspects of the helper stage niche remain intact as children get older. The Baka, Central African forest foragers, provide an illustrative and typical case. In this particular study, 95 percent of the sample children were involved in household maintenance:

> Baka children have the freedom to make their own decisions, but they are also considered responsible for the consequences of such decisions. Baka children are also expected to participate in daily household chores such as fetching water, bringing meals to neighboring households, or collecting firewood. However, very few obligations are imposed upon Baka children, and physical punishment is rare. (Gallois et al., 2015: 4)

Among the Runa, forager/farmers in the Ecuadorian Amazon:

> Children unanimously emphasized how accomplishing a task felt good because that caused someone else to [enjoy the benefit]. One boy described how he felt happy to have successfully hunted a tapir because that meant his mother would no longer be hungry [and] a young girl was proud when her manioc beer was served to [appreciative] guests and family members. (Mezzenzana, in press: 26–27)

Among the Araucanian (Chile):

> Praise and rewards were seldom given [to children]. To give a girl recognition for what she was, or did, was not the custom; the very fact that a parent was satisfied with her and with what she did, was enough reward. (Hilger, 1957: 77)

Hence, we see continuation in the autonomous and largely volunteer basis on which virtually *all* children contribute freely to the household economy.

In the next section, I review the antecedent period of the child's life history prior to becoming a helper.

2 Setting the Stage

The helper stage is an important period of development and change in human life history and involves other processes besides the emergence of helping. Several of these processes are inexorably linked to helping, however, and three are surveyed in this section. First is the often-dramatic transition from the predictable routines of infant care to the much more varied and less welcome

---

[4] Dahl (2015) posits a "social-interactionist" model of infant helping that is similar.

demands of the weaned or soon-to-be-weaned infant. An infant may be a welcome addition to the family, while a toddler may be a demanding burden. At the outset of the helper stage, therefore, the child may face a certain degree of social debt that can be reduced by coming to the aid of others.

As discussed in Section 2.2, sharing is paired with helping as altruistic or prosocial behavior and also emerges in early childhood. In spite of their complementarity, many societies treat helping as appearing automatically, while sharing must be taught or at least monitored and corrected as necessary.

Section 2.3 links play and helping. Like helping, play, particularly make-believe, is universal and often provides a kind of apprenticeship for the would-be helper. In village settings, play is focused largely on reenacting scenes from daily life, which, of course, are dominated by routine tasks in connection with the provision of food, clothing, and shelter – in a word, "work." The child may reach at least a rudimentary facility with various work-related tasks through play and thereby enhance their value as a helper.

2.1 Retiring Social Debt

Because of the newborn's vulnerability and the high value placed on fertility, infants are afforded a privileged position. They receive constant supervision by mothers and others 24/7. The mother "wears" her infant and begins nursing as soon as the child awakens. Others hold the infant, providing comfort and attention to their needs, including cleaning and safety. As a result of this period of complete dependency, children may be viewed as "moral debtors," as incurring what has been referred to as the "milk debt" (Millard & Graham, 1985: 72).

Consequently, when this intensive care is no longer seen as necessary and/or when a new, even-more-demanding baby is imminent, the child's position may be altered. Prothro (1961: 66) refers to the infant's "dethronement." Toddlers may fall to the bottom of the status hierarchy. As they lose their endearing vulnerability, toddlers may be identified more with their incompetence, lack of motor skills, undeveloped speech, and bad manners than with the many attractive traits of the infant. On Malaita Island (Melanesia), "children are pushed to be adults as soon as possible" (Watson-Gegeo & Gegeo, 2001: 3). Many societies delay the conferral of personhood (Lancy 2014) until children can more closely approximate adult behavior, especially as workers: "When a Nuer (South Sudan) boy 'tethers the cattle and herds the goats . . . when he cleans the byres and spreads the dung to dry and collects it and carries it to the fires he is considered a person'" (Evans-Pritchard, 1956: 146).

While the cavalier treatment of toddlers seems common and perfectly accep-table cross-culturally, among at least some societies, children are "indulged":

nursing is prolonged, and toddlers continue to receive care and attention from adults (Tronick, Morelli, & Ivey, 1992). In the majority of societies, however, adults tend to view older infants or toddlers as a burden, especially if the mother has become pregnant or recently given birth (Trivers, 1974). Toddlers are relegated to the care of less productive family members, such as grand-mothers and older siblings. This phenomenon is so widespread that the term "toddler rejection" was coined to describe it (Weisner & Gallimore, 1977: 176). Table 2.1 displays a sample of relevant cases.

Table 2.1 Withdrawing the infant's social support

"One of the most striking features in the Akan (Ghana) attitude to the child is the contrast between the lavish affection meted out to infants . . . and the harsh disregard which is the lot of most older children. The adored small child has to suffer the trauma of growing into an object of contempt" (Field, 1970: 28).

"The golden period of Maori (New Zealand) infancy invariably comes to an end with the birth of the next child. . . . The new baby claims the lion's share of the mothers' attention. He has novelty value, so it is he, and not the toddler, who is passed from knee to knee at social gatherings" (Ritchie, 1957: 83–5).

"Weaning is done when the baby is about one year old. . . . Alorese (Indonesia) weanlings cry, shriek, and kick in order to gain access to the breast . . . [they receive] frightening threats: 'If you continue nursing, the snakes will come or the toad will eat you.' Finally, the mother rubs her nipples with pepper or lemon" (Du Bois, 1941: 154).

"Gau Islanders (Fiji) . . . treat harshly any child who seems to be lagging behind in their developmental timetable . . . a fourteen-month-old that is still not walking will be given a chili-pepper enema" (Toren, 1990: 171).

A number of societies accelerate the transition to the toddler stage. !Kung (Botswana) foragers accelerate sitting, standing, and walking because "in the traditional mobile subsistence pattern . . . children who cannot walk constitute major burdens" (Konner, 1976: 290).

"Sulkiness, stubbornness, and tyrannical behavior, however, are short lived. The Taira (Taiwan) child finds that although this kind of behavior brought immediate and rewarding responses in the past, he now faces further withdrawal or punishment as a result" (Maretzki & Maretzki, 1963: 111).

"Between two and four years of age a Nurs (Iran) child is a girvaru – a habitually dissatisfied" individual whose whining is more often met with a beating than sympathy (Friedl, 1997: 124).

"An infant that cries and fusses until picked up, fed, changed, and so on, is acceptable; a whining, clinging, demanding toddler is not. While [Hawaiian] babies live in the midst of an adult world, indeed, often at its very center,

Table 2.1 (cont.)

toddlers are expected to function in a separate sphere that only overlaps with that of adults at the peripheries" (Gallimore, Boggs, & Jordan, 1974: 119).

"As [Samoan] babies approach the end of their first year, their crying is increasingly treated as a nuisance, rather than a cause for concern, and they are more likely to be shouted at or punished" (Ochs, 1988: 180).

The dramatic change in the child's status is found so reliably that I can suggest it as one of the legs on which the helper stage rests. Developmental psychology offers a sympathetic and complementary view. Rochat writes, "The fear of rejection [may lead to an] exacerbated need of humans to affiliate and bind to others [which] probably evolved as an adaptation to their extraordinary prolonged immaturity and helplessness outside the womb" (Rochat, 2009: 21, 25). Rohner (1986) claims that children need to feel "accepted" if they are not to suffer a socio-emotional deficit. Much earlier, McClelland (1961) had proposed a universal "need for affiliation," and psychological anthropologist Walter Goldschmidt (2006) posits the existence of "affect hunger."

It may be that volunteering to help provides a mechanism for the rejected toddler to re-affiliate with significant others. Perhaps infants who are "rejected" as toddlers may, effectively, "return to the nest" by being helpful to their mothers and other adult kin. Remaining in the proximity of the mother as an aide means one is never far from freshly gathered or prepared food, shelter, a warming fire, a comforting squeeze. Wynn sees the helper's clumsy overtures as a "promissory note" and pithily imagines the child's calculation: "'I can't actually be of measurable help yet, but see what a cooperative nature I have, and how genuinely helpful I'll be one day'" (Wynn, 2009: 483). But the helpful toddler does not exclusively target their ministrations to the mother. In the lab experiments discussed later in this section, fourteen-month-old children willingly offer to assist total strangers. Of course, in the village, "total strangers" are rare, and children's prosocial overtures are likely directed at close kin (Wynn, 2009) who may be more willing to comfort the youngster than their own mother.

I would again add the qualifier that among at least some foraging societies such as the Congolese Bofi (Fouts, 2005), toddlers continue to be "indulged" through being carried and nursed on demand until roughly three years of age. Perhaps as a consequence, helping may be less evident among the very young. In one seventeen-site survey based on spot observations of children's activities throughout the day, children in forager societies were found to log fewer hours of work per day (2.5–3 hours) *on average* than farming or pastoralist children (Kramer, 2019). And then there's WEIRD society, where children get a "free pass," perceived as a "gift" and a "joy" but never a burden – yet WEIRD toddlers volunteer to assist quite reliably.

Lowered expectations for helping among foragers may be offset by very high expectations for sharing. In the next subsection, I survey ethnographic literature that illustrates explicit lessons in sharing aimed at infants.

2.2 The Importance of Sharing

Helping and sharing often get rolled into the overarching "prosocial behavior." But recent research suggests that the two – sharing an altruistic foundation, and psychologically and culturally complementary – are, nevertheless, distinct. Unlike with helping, which (except in WEIRD society) is treated as inherent in the child's makeup and not requiring deliberate instruction, a number of societies intervene early to promote sharing (Aka (Congo) – Boyette, 2013: 126; Araucanian (Chile) – Hilger, 1957: 52; Wolof (Senegal) – Zempleni-Rabain, 1973: 227). And Boyette estimates that Aka socialization is effective: "Children, by four years old, are well accustomed to the idea that one must share and that there are implications for not sharing" (Boyette, 2019: 490). Generosity is demanded of very young Ngoni (Malawi) children – forcing them to donate prized resources to peers, for example (Read, 1960: 155). Most striking are the !Kung, who hold very low expectations for children as helpers but are quite anxious about children's commitment to sharing: "Like other hunter-gatherers, the !Kung are 'fierce egalitarians.'" They "consider refusal to share as the ultimate sin" (Howell 2010: 194). And, while teaching or other forms of active socialization are rare,

> Infants [are] taught about the importance of exchanging objects. They are brought into the formal system of reciprocity soon after birth, and between their sixth month and first year, their grandmother begins symbolic training in *hxaro* by guiding the giving of beads to relatives. Moreover, they are encouraged to share things, and their first words include *na* [give it to me] and *i* [here, take this]. (Bakeman et al., 1990: 796)

Table 2.2 displays an array of cases that illustrate the deliberate socialization of infants in sharing. While sharing is clearly critical in highly egalitarian hunting and gathering societies, it is very widely acknowledged as a virtue that requires cultivation in the very young. Taking the experimental literature into account, investigators have found that "At age 3–4, the overwhelming majority of children behave selfishly" and don't reliably share until age seven–eight (Fehr et al., 2008: 1079). This inherent and obvious selfishness on the part of infants is, I would argue, the prime motivator for those who feel compelled to train the very young to share.

Table 2.2 The importance of sharing

The Inuit take a *laissez-faire* stance toward their children's socialization: "Children are allowed to explore the world using what skills they can muster; and there is remarkably little meddling by older people in this learning process. Parents do not presume to teach their children what they can as easily learn on their own" (Guemple, 1979: 50). The exception involves sharing, which is "stressed by giving bits of food and toys to the baby and by eliciting gifts of these same items from it. This 'drill' in reciprocity goes on continuously" (Guemple, 1979: 43).

The Papel (Guinea-Bissau) engage older infants in a game of give and take. "The child will be offered an item, or a piece of food, but then asked to give it back. . . . If the child keeps the item, unwilling to share it with others, it will be commented on [or] hit lightly on its shoulder or cheek . . . a sign of disapproval of her or his unwillingness to share" (Einarsdóttir, 2004: 94).

"A Kaoka (Guadalcanal) toddler presented with a piece of fruit is told to give half to 'So-and-so,' and should the order be resisted, the adult ignores all protests and breaks a piece off to hand to the child's companion" (Hogbin, 1969: 33).

"In contrast to the casual learning of skills, certain values are more self-consciously inculcated [among the Great Whale Inuit]. . . . Lessons in sharing are given when the child is sent to beg a neighbor for tea, when gifts of meat or fish are sent out of the family" (Honigmann & Honigmann, 1953: 41).

"Aka children, by four years old, are well accustomed to the idea that one must share and [could expect] negative feedback to be a common response to selfishness. . . . As a mother shares out portions of a meal to family members, she will say 'Watch me, this is how to share. You will share like this. Take this to so-and-so'" (Boyette, 2019: 481, 490–1).

"Once Batek (Borneo) children could walk well, adults explicitly taught them to share food by handing them plates of food to deliver to other families" (Endicott & Endicott, 2008: 124).

Several points are worth noting. First, the literature in child psychology suggests the following: (1) "Young children's helping behavior is not potentiated or facilitated by parental behavior in the immediate situation, suggesting that it is spontaneous and intrinsically motivated" (Warneken & Tomasello, 2013: 345). Whereas, (2) "Toddlers are notoriously poor at sharing their possessions" (Svetlova, Nichols, & Brownell, 2010: 1818). If parents are anxious to ensure and even accelerate the child's prosociality, sharing may need a push, while helping may not.

A second point is that these lessons may not be necessary; children may learn the social norms governing sharing from observing and interacting with others. In an experimental study with samples drawn from six distinct societies, sharing rates did not vary cross-culturally until middle childhood, when "children tracked toward the behavior of adults in their own societies" (House et al., 2013: 1). Hadza (Tanzania) child foragers who have been systematically studied by Crittenden and others illustrate this.

While there is strong sanctioning of Hadza children should they fail to share, there are no explicit sharing lessons. Nevertheless, young, successful foragers – like their parents – willingly share their bounty, especially by middle childhood (Crittenden, 2016a). Among males, the small mammals they fell with bows and arrows are generally roasted and consumed on the spot – by a group of peers – regardless of individual success. Girls are more likely to bring any surplus from foraging (such as fruit) home to share with family. In a truly playful mind-set, groups of children collaborate in setting lures and traps for unwary weaverbirds. The captives are roasted and shared out, including to the youngest children who were not able to contribute to the harvest (Crittenden, 2016a, 2016b). Foraged foods are shared with kin and non-kin alike (Crittenden & Zes, 2015). One might infer from the Hadza studies that explicit socialization of sharing is probably unnecessary, and lab studies offer considerable support: "We found that young 3-year-old children inferred normativity without any normative language and without any pedagogical cues" (Schmidt, Rakoczy, & Tomasello 2011: 530).

Third, the model of child help presented to this point is actually a somewhat better fit with societies that rely on cultivation and herding.[5] In these subsistence systems, a great deal of the work is done collaboratively, and the work often provides varying sub-tasks that can be matched to the size and skill of the participants, including helpers; whereas, among hunters and gatherers, the work may be carried out individually. Gathering, such as digging tubers or picking fruit, even when undertaken in a mixed-age group, is executed by individuals. Similarly, hunting and trapping, the domain of men and boys, is often done solo (Rival, 2002; Boyette, 2013). One implication is that affiliation-seeking children in a foraging community may gain social capital not only through pitching-in but also through sharing their bounty: "When the Buton (Sulawesi) child practices angling on the reef flat, he is catching fish that are consumed by [the] household, and this serves, at least in part, as his motivation" (Vermonden, 2009: 218).

Among the Ese Eja of the Peruvian Amazon,

> [W]hat I mostly see are children independently fishing, gathering, etc. – and individually taking this home – not necessarily helping their mothers or fathers hunt or fish. The little ones bring the tiniest little fish (equivalent to

---

[5] A series of photos shared with me by colleague Tian Xiaojie (personal communication, June 1, 2019) shows Maasai (Tanzania) children across a broad age range (three to fifteen) assisting with the corralling and sorting of livestock for pasturing, watering, and branding, during which they keep very young sheep and goats separated from the herd.

Figure 2.1 Turtle Eggs to Share (Peru: Daniela Peluso)

one swallow) but they are treated as though they are large. (Daniela Peluso, personal communication, June 6, 2019)

Laura Rival notes from the Huaorani (Ecuador), "Nothing is more cheering for a parent than a three-year-old's decision to join a food gathering expedition. The child carries his/her own *oto* (basket) . . . and brings it back to the longhouse filled with forest products to 'give away,' that is, to share with co-residents" (Rival, 2000: 116).

Outside of WEIRD society, children everywhere show a readiness to assist others or share their foraged resources, and investigators have no difficulty identifying, coding, and tallying the considerable amount of time children spend working. Of course, these same observation studies reveal that work hours are matched or exceeded by play. Regardless of subsistence type, all children play during the helper stage and later. But, as I will show in the next subsection, much of that play is work-themed.

2.3 Playing at Work

Whittemore (1989: 92) identifies key elements of the transition from infancy to toddlerhood among the Mandinka (West Africa): "With the arrival of the next sibling, infancy is over. Now, play begins and membership in a social group of peers is taken to be critical to *nyinandirangho*, the forgetting of the breast to which the toddler has had free access for nearly two years or more. As one mother put it, 'Now she must turn to play.'" But, unlike their WEIRD counter-parts, whose play often involves invented or fantasy characters and scenarios (Power, 2000; Gaskins, 2013), Mandinka toddlers will be immersed in the real world, even as they are playing.

Before children can contribute in any useful way as helpers, their play is oriented toward work. Toddlers who "play pound" (in Africa, a large mortar and pestle are commonly employed in processing grain and other comestibles, and children simulate these tools and actions) will, in a short while, be pounding for real, assisting an older sister perhaps (Bock & Johnson, 2004).

Figure 2.2 Using a Mortar and Pestle (Peru: Daniela Peluso)

Table 2.3 Play and work intertwined

Separating Bonerate (Sulawesi) children's "work from play is often problematic" (Broch, 1990: 83).
"In fact, one of the most striking aspects of [East-Central Sudanese] children's lives was the fusion between the activities of work, play and learning. . . . Knowledge acquired in the course of children's participation in work was reinforced and enhanced in their play" (Katz, 1986: 47).
"It is exactly the interweaving of play and work [by Bamana (Mali) children] that is striking" (Polak, 2012: 96).
Among Pygmy (Congo) societies, "there is not the same distinction between work and play that exists in the west" (Boyette, 2016: 161).
"After watching 3- to 4-year-old Hadza (Tanzania) playing a while, one eventually realizes that children are not just playing but are actually digging small tubers and eating them. . . . Foraging simply emerges gradually from playing" (Marlowe, 2010: 156).

Before they can join an outrigger sailing crew, would-be Ifaty (Madagascar) sailors are learning to be nimble through playing on and in a beached craft (Lancy, 2015b).

This finding of the merging of play and work is one of the earliest and most widespread in the ethnographic record. It suggests to me that even though very young children seem devoted to play, the "content" of their play often, or mostly, reflects the work that's going on around them. Table 2.3 provides affirmation from several ethnographers across a varied range of societies.

The "practice" or "trying on" quality of make-believe is not limited to discrete skills but also includes the full gamut of social behaviors and speech associated with the activity they are imitating. There is often explicit recognition by adults in the community and visiting anthropologists that children at play are preparing for work. For example, adults are generally quite liberal when it comes to children "borrowing" their tools to "use." When challenged by the ethnographer pointing out the danger inherent in sharp-edged blades of various kinds, parents are likely to respond with, "But how else can they learn to use the tool?" (Lancy, 2016a). Somewhat less frequent are reports of adults supplying children with scaled down but usable versions of common tools to practice with (Lew-Levy et al., 2019) or use in "object" play. As examples, among the Penan of Borneo, "play is a very important means of acquiring skills, which . . . parents encourage by making smaller-sized weapons, such as spears and blowpipes, for children to practice with" (Puri, 2005: 282). "Fais Island (Micronesia) boys learn to fish with child-sized poles made for them" (Rubenstein, 1979: 185).

Another frequently noted aspect of the village play group, in which older children both care for their younger siblings and also involve them in work-themed play, is the seamless transition from playing at working to working while playing. The play group becomes, imperceptibly, a work group (see Figure 2.2).

Baka children who might, on another occasion, be engaged in "play," routinely collaborate in weir fishing. The older children cut down branches and dig up clods of soil, and very small children carry these to the site where the diversion dam will be constructed. Once the weir is constructed, younger children walk the stream bed, driving fish into the trap, where older children harvest them. Once the dam collapses, the children gather to clean and divide up their catch – maintaining a cheerful, spontaneous atmosphere throughout (Hagino & Yamauchi, 2016). The young Mbya Guarani (Argentina) child will be exposed to new environments beyond the immediate vicinity of the village, as they tag along with their sib caretakers to the forest adjacent to the village to gather ripe fruits (Remorini, 2016). Mikea children in Madagascar forage "because it is an enjoyable social activity . . . an extension of play that occurs outside camp" (Tucker & Young, 2005: 168):

> Foraging of the young is for the Zafimaniry (Madagascar) an adventurous but not a serious form of activity . . . a form of play. Consequently, the product of such activity, although it is very important nutritionally and economically, is not, nor in their evaluation should it be, taken seriously. (Bloch, 1988: 28)

Quite recently, several studies strongly reinforce the idea that play acts as a kind of "holding pattern" for children who are anxious to help but are not quite "ready." Lew-Levy and Boyette (2018) have done a very important time-allocation study among Aka forager and Ngandu farmer children in the Congo Basin. They found that, as expected, children play less and work more as they age; but unexpectedly, at every age sampled, from three to sixteen, children from both communities allocate more time to work than to play. Fouts et al. (2016: 687) found that children from another Central African forest forager community prefer to use real tools, including knives (when available), in their make-believe play. Even earlier, Gaskins (1999) found that Yucatec Mayan toddlers were already spending more time observing work or doing it than they spent in play:

> [T]he extensive time Yucatec Mayan children spend in playing is not an indication they value play above work, but, rather, that their work abilities remain marginal and they turn to play when they are excluded from work. . . . Thus, although play is a significant activity in children's lives, it is not the most highly valued even for children as young as four. (Gaskins, Haight, & Lancy, 2007: 193)

These findings from field studies have received support from recent US studies (Taggart, Heise, & Lillard, 2017; Taggart et al., 2018). A sample of 100 children, aged three to six, was asked to choose between pretend and real versions of nine activities, and justifications for their choices were recorded. When given a choice, preschool-age children overwhelmingly preferred real activities to their pretend equivalents – 65 percent to 35 percent. Sixty-nine percent preferred to bake actual cookies rather than pretend to make cookies; 60 percent preferred to cut real vegetables with a paring knife; 66 percent preferred actual fishing; 74 percent preferred to feed a live baby; and so on. Children's preference for real activities appeared between three and four years of age, then was constant through age six. Children said they preferred real activities because they are functional and useful and provide novel experiences. When children preferred pretend activities, the most cited reasons were being afraid of the real, lack of ability, and lack of permission. I believe that the WEIRD child-rearing model has misled parents (and professionals) into thinking that children prefer play over work or that play is somehow more appropriate for them (Lancy, 2017a).

These studies illustrate very young children's eagerness to get involved with "real" adult activities by pitching in or endeavoring to be helpful. However, I would say that make-believe and object play have a significant role in helping focus children's attention on work and afford them the means to try out and practice more mature activities while avoiding the conflict that arises when clumsy, incompetent, would-be helpers are rebuffed. I want to suggest that as children transition from playing to working, the doorway between the two should have a sign that says "Helpers Welcome Here." The child enters the helper stage motivated by an accumulation of social debt as well as playful experience that more and more closely matches tasks they may well volunteer to assist with.

3 Weighing the Evidence

Throughout this Element, I weave together evidence of many kinds and drawn from distinct epistemological traditions. Anthropology offers a kind of patchwork quilt of data types. Prominent is the *ethnographic* study in which the anthropologist is a resident observer for an extended period in an obscure, small-scale, face-to-face community. From the beginning, observation and detailed notes on what one observes/hears are the core data. The observer communicates in the native tongue and cultivates relationships with individuals who become "informants" – reliable, articulate interpreters to whom the ethnographer can turn for help in completing, correcting, and interpreting the raw recordings of scenes and speech. Photographs and audio/video recordings add another layer of data to one's notes but also require interpretation and annotation. More formal data collection might include "spot observation," where, by systematic time sampling, the investigator can calculate relative frequencies of specific behaviors. In the study of childhood, time allocated to work versus play is frequently measured. Interviews may be formalized to varying degrees – from asking the same questions of a specified sample of subjects to more informal interviewing of individuals one has come to know intimately. Interviews with children are particularly problematic because of a natural shyness toward outsiders, and also because adults do not routinely seek information or opinions from children. It is customary for the ethnographer to write up their study in a relatively lengthy monograph. The great length enables the writer to provide detailed descriptions from field notes as well as verbatim transcriptions of recorded speech. The author does not stop at detailing the phenomenon of interest but adds context to firmly embed it in the larger culture. In many respects, this step is the essential achievement. Vivid anecdotes and texts drawn from field notes add credibility to the ethnographer's analyses and conclusions.

The anthropological study of childhood is challenged by the paucity of studies that focus specifically on children. To achieve a reasonably comprehensive survey of childhood across a great variety of ethnically distinct communities requires mining the entire ethnographic corpus for material that illuminates the experience of juveniles. So, while no more than two dozen monographs focus on juveniles, children play at least a cameo role in several hundred reports (Lancy, 2015b). I have found particularly valuable accounts that reveal the ethnographer's surprise and even shock at adult behavior toward children revealing a dramatic contrast with the ethnographer's culturally formed expectations. Accompanied by his spouse during his research on childhood among the Dusun in North Borneo, T. R. Williams reports:

> We were faced daily with Dusun parents raising their children in ways that violated the basic beliefs by which we were raised. ... We consistently checked our ... exclamations of concern or disgust ... and [resisted] the temptation to take a "dangerous" object, such as a knife, from a toddler ... knowing that in terms of the local culture, children are believed to die from accidents whether they play with knives or not and besides, as one Dusun father put it, "How can you learn to use a knife if you do not use it." (Williams, 1969)

The process whereby these sources are located, annotated, collated, and analyzed is referred to as *ethnology* (Voget, 1975). The investigator conducting such a survey may approach the material deductively, whereby the questions are formulated in advance, or inductively, by letting the pattern emerge from the data-mining process. With respect to the study of child helpers, the approach has been largely inductive.

I will provide a brief survey of child helping in the ethnographic record, followed by a parallel survey of studies carried out within the traditions of experimental child psychology. This research stands in direct contrast to what I have just described. Far from elaborately contextualizing the child as helper, the experimental study of helping will decontextualize the behavior, reducing it to its essentials. Context or other aspects that may already be familiar to particular children add "noise" to the data, making the behavior harder to interpret. While care may be taken in selecting samples to control for variation by age and gender, thought is not often given to the influence of culture – exceptions noted later in the subsection. That is, samples are drawn almost exclusively from WEIRD (Henrich et al., 2010) communities. Lab experiments are, without exception, deductive, with hypotheses stated in advance. In the conduct of the experiment, every attempt is made to standardize the experience. Sessions are typically quite short, and the adults who are to serve as the beneficiaries of the child's help are carefully trained to behave consistently. Verbal interaction is tightly scripted.

In one of the earlier lab studies (Warneken & Tomasello, 2007), twenty-seven middle-class German children, aged around fourteen months, were selected. Three were excluded for "fussiness." Parents were present but remained unengaged. A trained experimenter (E) carried out six tasks in front of the child and, in the process, had some difficulty: he drops a clothespin but cannot reach it; he does the same with a marker; he loses a spoon in a hole and cannot recover it because his hand is too large; and he has a pile of books to stow in a cabinet but does not have a hand free to open the door. The experimenter does not verbalize or indicate by glance or gesture that he seeks the child's assistance. Nor does E provide feedback following a helpful act. Mixed in with the *experimental* trials were *control* trials, where E acted on the same objects used in the experimental trials. The control trials had E throw the clothespin or marker on the floor, as examples. The sessions were video recorded, and then a naïve (unaware of the aims of the study) assistant coded the child's behavior. The majority of the children very quickly saw the problem and intervened appropriately, at least in the simpler tasks where the lost object was out of reach. Only a very few helping responses were made in the control trials.

This study represents the typical paradigm where individual children, without guidance, witness an adult (E) experience a problem in completing a simple task – a problem that the child might be able to solve. The child views this event in real time, and their subsequent behavior is video recorded. The video will be later coded and the data aggregated and analyzed for trends relevant to the stated hypotheses. I now turn to brief surveys of the relevant ethnography, followed by laboratory studies. In comparing these two "ways of knowing," I am in agreement with Ashley Maynard's dictum "fieldwork first, experiments later" (Maynard 2006; see also Gurven & Winking 2008).

3.1 Helping in the Ethnographic Record

Descriptions of child helpers are common in the ethnographic record. Quite recently, in her study of Runa (Ecuador) children, Mezzenzana recorded an episode of a three-year-old boy volunteering to help a neighbor butcher a tapir: "He was not asked to help and yet, the little child had come forward with water and a knife and assisted the woman throughout the process" (in press).

The sample cases in Table 3.1 were selected because they reveal (with added italics) the eagerness and joy that accompanies children's efforts to pitch in.

Table 3.1 Helping across the ethnographic record

"Among Mayo (Mexico) villagers, little girls target their mother's task inventory, selecting one within their capacity, like bringing water from the arroyo – 'a little girl *begs* to undertake new tasks'" (Erasmus, 1955: 331).

"During the rice harvest season, whole Taira (Taiwan) families are involved. Even a little child . . . stands by *gloomily* until an adult hands him a small bundle of sheaves to carry to the threshers" (Maretzki & Maretzki, 1963: 510).

"Mixtecan (Mexico) children are *happy* when they're performing 'little tasks' for adults" (Romney & Romney, 1963: 573).

Little Talensi (Ghana) boys are said to possess "a *passionate* desire to raise a hen" (Fortes, 1938/1970: 20).

"Bamana (Mali) children's desire to participate in the adults' work-life is *overwhelming*" (Polak, 2012: 110).

Chaga (East Africa) "children *delight* in . . . cleaning out the animals' quarters . . . [they] ask for permission to [help] their mothers carry out the dung" (Raum, 1940: 199).

"Three-year-old Gusii (Kenya) children volunteer to hoe alongside their mothers and appear to *enjoy* it very much" (LeVine & LeVine, 1963: 182).

"A Mazahua child shows an *impatient readiness* for adult behavior" (Paradise, 1987: 180).

Himalayan (Uttarakhand, India) pastoralist children said they feel "a type of internal *compulsion* to work" (Dyson, 2014: 43).

Note: Italics added in all cases.

Note in these excerpts the emotionally laden descriptors of young helpers' states of mind.

In virtually every ethnographic study that gives any attention to children, child helpers will be noted – from participant observations, from interviews with parents and caretakers (extolling the importance of child helpers), and from focused empirical studies aiming to measure and codify children's activities. In striking contrast to this rich and consistent picture of child helpers across cultural and historical accounts of childhood, children as helpers, until recently, are largely absent from mainstream developmental psychology.[6] I selected a convenient sample of five reference works on child development published by top academic presses, including Oxford University Press, Cambridge University Press, and the University of Chicago Press (Haith & Benson, 2008; Shweder et al., 2009; Goldstein & Naglieri, 2011; Britto, Engle, & Super, 2013; Hopkins, Geangu, & Linkenauger, 2017). These volumes range in length from 506 to 2,200 pages. Over all five volumes, there was no mention of or reference to the child as helper. Not one. This lack of scholarly interest is mirrored in popular opinion. WEIRD parents were asked to rank the value of various manifestations of prosocial behavior in their two- and five-year-olds. "Happy" and "cheerful" topped the list. "Helpful" was not in the top ten (Bergin, Bergin, & French, 1995).

In the vast body of research and theory on child development conducted within WEIRD societies, children are not helpers; they are helped – by parents, teachers, coaches, policies, treatments, lessons, and so on. However, as I will now discuss, recent research by Warneken and others has begun to rectify this omission.

3.2 Lab Studies of Child Helpers

As cross-cultural researchers are particularly aware, there is often a sharp disconnect between findings "from the field" and findings from lab studies with WEIRD populations (LeVine, 2007; Lancy, 2015b). A noteworthy exception occurs with respect to recent research on children helping. This line of lab research is essential to my claim that there is a helper stage in human life history. As varied and pervasive as accounts of child helpers are in the ethnographic record, the lab studies are crucial. They show that subjects as young as fourteen months, and possibly earlier, are eager to be helpful. The precision in measuring age and the large sample sizes are not available to the anthropologist studying children in a traditional rural village. The decontextualized settings created in

---

[6] In sixteenth- to twentieth-century workshops and factories, unwaged younger children "helped" older family members, thereby increasing their output and earnings (Horn 1994).

the lab greatly reduce the likelihood that this behavior is "learned." However, it can never be claimed that the influence of culture or learning is reduced to zero. The experiments themselves are a product of WEIRD culture after all.

What follows in this subsection summarizes the critical findings from a research program undertaken by Felix Warneken and colleagues. In multiple studies, fourteen+/–month-old children, as long as they had some sense of what was needed, consistently volunteered to help. And they offered assistance "before the adult either looked to them or verbalized his problem ... and eye contact (as a subtle means of soliciting help) was also unnecessary ... nor were they ever rewarded or praised for their effort" (Warneken & Tomasello, 2007: 279).

The progress of lab research on child helpers has continued to "push the envelope," so to speak – adding chimpanzees as subjects and varying the experimental paradigm to make helping more challenging. For example, eighteen-month-old children forgo the opportunity to play with novel toys to go to the aid of an adult completing a task. They will also traverse an obstacle course to reach the person needing assistance (Warneken & Tomasello, 2009). On the other hand, "children who received a toy for helping were subsequently less likely to help spontaneously than children who had never been 'paid'" (Warneken, 2015b: 2). The authors conclude that "toddlers are instinctively altruistic (unlike chimps; Melis et al., 2011) and providing them with extrinsic rewards for their assistance actually diminishes their ardor" (Warneken & Tomasello, 2009: 460). Warneken finds that children volunteer even when "there may be no immediate expectation of reciprocity" (Warneken, 2015a).

Children are proactive, intervening with help even when the adult is unaware there's a problem. They "differentiate intention from accident, intervening only if the outcome does not match the person's presumed goal ... they do this without anyone asking for help or explaining the problem" (Warneken, 2015b: 1). They will offer assistance, like retrieving a dropped item, even when the adult is unaware of a problem (Warneken, 2013: 101).

On the other hand, they are often able to decode the situation and then offer assistance *only when it is required **and** they are capable of assisting* (Warneken, 2015b). Additional findings are shown in Table 3.2.

Historically, the presumed core psychological mechanism underlying prosocial behavior, which includes helping, has been "empathic concern." This is the vicarious affective response that results from witnessing another person's distress. According to Hoffman (2000), empathy drives prosocial behavior. However, the evidence from Warneken's research does not support this view: "Situational helping behavior based on shared intentions provides an alternative

Table 3.2 Lab studies of children being helpful

Six-month-old infants were shown animated cartoons of a red ball struggling to roll up a hill, either helped by a yellow triangle or obstructed by a blue square shoving it back. The infants looked longer and were more likely to reach toward the helpful symbol (Hamlin, Wynn, & Bloom, 2007).

"Having parents present and offering encouragement did not influence 24-month-old children who consistently assisted a strange adult trying to obtain an out-of-reach object . . . helping behavior is not potentiated or facilitated by parental behavior in the immediate situation, suggesting that it is spontaneous and intrinsically motivated" (Warneken & Tomasello, 2013: 245).

"Children younger than 5 years do not seem to be concerned by whether they are being watched or acting in private, indicating that reputational effects are not foundational for prosocial behaviors" (Warneken, 2015b: 2).

" [C]hildren can help by correcting a person's course of action . . . when a person requested a nonfunctional object (such as a cup with a hole), 3-year-olds handed over an intact object instead. Similarly, when an adult was unaware that a toy was no longer in the box he was struggling to open, 18-month-olds did not assist with opening that box but fetched the object from the correct location" (Warneken, 2015b: 2).

"Young children make these inferences based on minimal cues. Specifically, children often help without anyone asking for help or explaining the problem . . . verbal and nonverbal communication is unnecessary" (Warneken, 2015b: 1).

When given a choice, three-year-olds preferentially offer to help friends rather than strangers (Engelmann, Haux, & Herrmann, 2019), strengthening the claim that children seek affiliation through helping.

Young children from [villages on Tanna Island, Vanuatu] take action to intervene on another's behalf, "even in the absence of concurrent behavioral or communicative cues indicating that help is necessary" (Aime et al., 2017).

The conviction that child helping is universal and therefore heritable is reinforced by the findings from lab studies indicating, under optimum circumstances, that our nearest relatives, "chimpanzees share the motivation and skills necessary to help others" (Melis et al., 2011: 1405).

Nevertheless, "children are much earlier, more flexible and proactive helpers than chimpanzees. While active sharing is rare among chimpanzees overall, young children share the spoils of their joint labor" (Melis & Warneken, 2016: 302).

---

explanation for toddlers' prosocial behavior" (Kärtner et al., 2010: 905). Another recent study concludes that child subjects in the lab studies of helping appear to be engaged in "instrumental helping – defined as behavior that is intended to fulfill others' goal-directed needs. This kind of behavior is often interpreted as the first instance of human cooperation" (Giner Torréns & Kärtner, 2017: 353).

A recent neuroimaging study also confirms the distinction between instrumental and empathic interventions:

> Different neurophysiological patterns predicted the emergence of helping and comforting: Empathic responding and comforting were related to left-centered frontal activation asymmetries, a marker of emotional processing, whereas instrumental helping was related to right-centered temporal asymmetry, probably reflecting task- and goal-related understanding. (Paulus, 2014: 79)

And from the ethnographic record as well, child helpers seem more interested in contributing to the accomplishment of a goal than in demonstrating empathy.

The lab studies just surveyed support an evolutionary basis for an early period or stage in the child's development when they reliably and sensibly provide assistance. This claim is made in view of the early onset, ubiquity, persistence in the face of obstacles, and the untutored and unguided sophistication of children's help. There is increasing evidence that children's helping involves not only the desire to help another but also an array of cognitive abilities that facilitate the child's decoding the situation to determine whether help would be welcome, the nature of help that might be called for, and a self-assessment of one's ability to help. These studies show a clear developmental effect where eighteen-month-olds are more capable than fourteen-month-olds in deconstructing situations that are more complex and "the propensity to respond pro-socially grows significantly between 18 and 30 months of age" (Svetlova et al., 2010: 1824).

Of course, there are many rough edges to this match between lab psychology and community ethnography (Rai & Fiske 2010). For example, the lab paradigms are limited to brief, one-shot episodes of helping, contrasted with the more complex and extended helping that occurs when children volunteer to assist with various family enterprises, like food preparation. To date, lab studies have focused on the very young, and any changes in the reliability or nature of the drive to be helpful – in short, evidence for the end of the helper stage – must come from anthropology.

4 Contrasting Cultural Contexts for Child Helpers

This Element grew out of a stark contradiction provoked by two unrelated lines of research. On the one hand was the lab research, reviewed earlier, showing a universal tendency for the very young to insistently offer help to others. On the other hand, a growing body of ethnographic research on WEIRD society (echoed in the popular press, parenting blogs, how-to manuals, etc.) painted a consistent picture of extremely resistant and unhelpful children from around six years of age. In this section, I attempt to resolve this paradox. The basic argument is that the helper stage provides a starting point for the transformation of juveniles into reliable workers in the family economy. Most societies provide a bridge (or scaffolding; Dahl, 2015) to facilitate this gradual transformation, whereas such a bridge may be unavailable in WEIRD families.

4.1 Sustaining the Drive to Be Helpful

Helping is universal (excepting, perhaps, the !Kung studied by Draper, 1975) and appears in societies throughout the ethnographic record including those where there are few, if any, demands on older children to carry out chores. In the WEIRD lab studies reviewed earlier, situations were somewhat artificial and tightly scripted. Outside WEIRD society, the would-be helper is handled quite differently in various cultural contexts (Giner Torréns & Kärtner, 2017). Generally speaking, helping is considered a voluntary act. Children can choose which activities to get involved in, and their efforts are typically accepted – within limits. As helpers, they also may elect to not participate or may tire of the activity and run off to play. Ju/'hoansi (Botswana) children, for example, often pitch in to fetch water or firewood, process mongongo nuts and animal hides, and prepare meals, but "it is well understood that children do these chores only if they feel like it" (Howell, 2010: 31). Among the Chiga (Tanzania), "the assumption of work and responsibility comes about gradually, and largely on the child's own initiative. This respect for the individual and his right to make work choices underlies Chiga treatment of young children throughout" (Edel, 1996: 178).

The most commonly observed settings that attract would-be helpers are public or semi-public work sites. Figures 4.1 and 4.2 illustrate very well a widespread and typical pattern where the child takes the initiative to become involved and, as de Haan notes, adults willingly accommodate them as partners. They "create room" (de Haan, 2001: 188) for them – obviously akin to the widespread custom of "making room at the dinner table." Note the circular arrangement in both photos. These mixed-age/mixed-ability work circles are common in the ethnographic record, and archaeologists have found them from the European Neolithic and earlier (Lancy, 2017b).

Not only is the child making an authentic contribution to the collective effort but, as both figures show, there is also physical contact among participants. This physical closeness may be especially welcomed by "rejected" toddlers.

Children inevitably gather around work sites to observe, listen, and if permitted help out. Butchering is typical of the activities that draw in helpers who

Figure 4.1 Family harvesting cáñere (Boivia: M. Ruth Martínez-Rodríguez)

Figure 4.2 Turtle-butchering party (Madagascar: David F. Lancy)

are largely tolerated, even if their help slows down the process. Nayaka (India) children assist in the butchering and the division of large game while learning a variety of technical skills and social and cultural norms:

> They gathered vessels or plantain leaves and brought them to where the meat was cut; they held a torch if the butchering took place at night; they held the animal's limbs to ease its cutting; they ... monitored the equal distribution of meat chunks ... and then carried the portions to the families. (Bird-David, 2015: 96; see also Sonoda, 2016)

But what happens when children's participation is unwelcome, typically because they might interfere with the work at hand: spilling grain, disturbing the hunter's or fisher's quarry, or forcing the worker to alter or slow their production to accommodate the would-be helper? Among seminomadic Mongol pastoralists, inept helpers are halted by a commonly used injunction: "'*Chi cbadabgui!*' – 'you can't do it!' [which] may be interpreted by children more as a challenge than a command" (Michelet, 2016: 236). In a Tstosil Maya (Mexico) community, a child's overtures to fit in may be initially rejected as a "deliberate provocation" to encourage skill improvement and social responsibility (Martínez-Pérez, 2015). Similarly, on Truk Island in Micronesia, rebuffed children redouble their efforts to become fully competent (Gladwin & Sarason, 1953).

Medaets (2016) describes the "stop, you can't do it!" phenomenon in villages on the Tapajós River in Brazil: "In the Tapajós region, adult experts do not automatically welcome the novice as a co-participant and may actually disparage and discourage children's attempts to demonstrate their emerging skills" (Medaets, 2016: 253). Responding negatively to a child's initial attempts at helping may act as a goad, leading to greater self-reliance. And the Tapajós child *will* be welcomed as a participant at the successful conclusion of their self-instruction.

These ethnographic observations are reinforced by a lab study in the United States that found that three- to six-year-old children who have experienced some ostracism are more diligent at copying a model. The study authors speculate that "imitation serves an affiliative function in response to the threat of ostracism" (Watson-Jones et al., 2014: 204; for similar results from Vanuatu (Melanesia), see Clegg & Legare, 2016: 1435).

Outright rejection is, however, rare. As Mead notes for Samoa (Polynesia): "[Samoan] children are never told they are 'too little,' 'too weak,' 'not old enough' to do anything. ... If a child attempts something beyond its capacity it will be diverted, but not openly discouraged" (Mead, 1967: 235–6). Barbara Polak describes a well documented case that illustrates the subtle management of the helper stage for the Bamana of Mali. The Bamana are fairly typical of farming communities in the Sahel:

Figure 4.3 Learning to hoe (Mali: Barbara Polak)

> Four-year-old Bafin has already grasped the meaning of sowing and is able to
> perform the various movements ... he is entrusted with an old hoe as well as
> with some seeds so that he can gain some practice in this activity.
> However ... he has to be allocated a certain part of the field where he neither
> gets in the way of the others nor spoils the rows they have already sown. ...
> As a rule, his rows have to be re-done. (Polak, 2003: 126, 129)

Bafin is, no doubt, inspired by seeing his siblings engaged in planting and
harvesting:

> [At harvest] three-year-old Daole ... begins to pluck beans from the tendrils.
> After he has filled the lid with a handful of beans, his interest fades. [He]
> carelessly leaves the lid with the beans lying on the ground and goes looking
> for some other occupation. ... Five-year-old Sumela ... looks out for a corner not
> yet harvested and picks as many beans as will fill his calabash ... [he] keeps on
> doing this for more than one and a half hours. ... Eleven-year-old Fase has been
> busy harvesting beans ... since morning. He works as fast as ... his father and
> grown-up brother ... and only takes a rest when they [do]. ... Fase is fully
> competent ... with regard to harvesting beans. He even takes on the role of
> supervising his younger brothers and checks their performance from time to time.
> (Polak, 2003: 130, 132).

We see here an instance of Weisner's notion of "chains of support," in which
each member of the family work group supports and guides those who are
slightly less advanced on the competency scale (Weisner, 1989: 78). In any
work party, older siblings often supervise children in the helper stage. And the

parents intervene rarely but strategically. A mother, for example, might take note that a little boy engaged in planting is getting tired – and in danger of carelessly damaging a furrow – so she sends him back to the village to fetch a gourd of water (Polak, 2012: 100).

The Bamana mother selects from a menu of child-appropriate tasks to redirect a child without denying them the opportunity to help. Errand running is a frequent choice: "Even [Hadza] youngsters who are still walking very unsteadily on their feet are conscripted by adults to hand knives, beads, and food to other nearby adults" (Crittenden, 2016a: 66). And, as numerous ethnographers have noted, the utilitarian task of errand running also serves to socialize the child to proper forms of interaction and address vis-à-vis neighbors, near and distant kin, adults of different ages, and so on: "The child is given the responsibility to learn through this task the accomplishments the society values" (Lee, 1967: 56).

Providing appropriate chores for juveniles can be seen as a form of moral socialization. The three cases that follow are representative:

> Giriama [Kenyan farmers] attach importance to providing children with duties that teach responsibility and mutuality. In their view, a mother who does not expect her children to help is remiss, even neglectful. A child so treated would inevitably emerge as an adult with few prospects and without the respect of the community (Wenger, 1989: 93).
>
> In a Yucatec Maya village, a parent does not hesitate to interrupt a child's play to assign a chore. From an early age, Mayan children are aware that work trumps play. "As the child grows older their inner energy and curiosity ... should be directed ... toward productive work" (Gaskins et al., 2007: 191).
>
> In many contexts in Jajikon (Micronesia), elders are supposed to "send" children to do things and make them work for their family ... this work benefits the child as well. ... Children who are not sent, adults told me "would not know how to work" or "how to live" (Berman, 2019: 110–11).

Also of note are brief tactical interventions that adults make to ease the child over an obstacle to the completion of a task. Examples include a father briefly assisting a boy with the correct position of the adze during canoe making (Wilbert, 1976), an adult making a correction in a fish trap a boy has made on his own (Vermonden, 2009), and a mother helping remove a stone blocking her daughter's digging stick from prying out a tuber (Boesch, 2013).

The helper stage establishes a pattern of relationships between the juvenile worker and their kin, which continues into adolescence. In a timely manner, family members provide resources and at least minimal guidance to the maturing worker:

> Navaho (US Southwest) children learn responsibility by being given indispensable household tasks; in addition, they are given sheep of their own from

the time they are about five. They are responsible for the care and welfare of these animals ... [and, hence] they can take their turn at supplying the meat for the family meal, and they can contribute mutton when this is needed for ceremonials or to entertain visitors" (Lee, 1961: 11).

A four- or five-year-old Mazahua (Mexico) girl ... spends hours, days, and weeks seated beside her mother or other women emulating and helping at an onion stand in the marketplace in México. She trims onions. She tirelessly practices tying them into bunches with or without success. She arranges them carefully on a piece of plastic laid out on the ground, fanning away insects patiently [until] eventually [she has] an opportunity to put together her own small stand (Paradise & Rogoff, 2009: 118). She learns "marketing ... by becoming directly involved in the various tasks implied and by taking the initiative and responsibility for learning without looking for or expecting instruction or helpful intervention from others" (Paradise, 1987: 10).

Most Kaoka (Melanesia) fathers have allocated at least one pig to the son by the time he is about eight; moreover, they insist that he accept full obligation to gather and husk coconuts each day so that the animal can be fed in the evening (Hogbin, 1969: 39).

In the Murik Lakes region of PNG, girls who've helped to dig clams are allocated a "share that is kept separate throughout the process of preparing them for market, and the amount of money earned from their harvest is given directly to them. ... By responding ... to children's efforts to help with work, mothers encourage a strong association between work, recognition, and being fed that is evident in many situations" (Barlow, 1985: 87).

Batek (Borneo) boys may also be independent rattan collectors, with the right to keep and dispose of any of their own proceeds (Lye, 1997: 363).

While children may enjoy a great deal of autonomy vis-à-vis domestic chores, even in the most indulgent communities, such as Aka pygmies (Congo), interviewed children acknowledged that all had served as infant minders, and there were consequences for refusing this chore, such as being denied food or "getting hit by the mother of the infant" (Boyette, 2019: 488).

Notwithstanding the cross-cultural and intra-individual variability in systems for accommodating eager young helpers, there is no case in the ethnographic record where the services of young helpers are simply dispensed with altogether. This clearly *is* the case in WEIRD society, and this antipathy toward child workers is unique. It is not that WEIRD toddlers do not offer to participate; they do, but they are diverted to other activities, reinforced by a full toy box and a library of juvenile video entertainment (Lancy, 2017a). As in the village, WEIRD children may be encouraged to engage in make-believe cooking, construction, infant care, and house cleaning, but these play-work activities transition to more sophisticated forms of recreation rather than to real work. In the ethnographic record, the participation of children, including the youngest, in family projects is commonplace. In WEIRD culture, by contrast, scenes of parents helping children with *their* personal agendas are far more common than the reverse. In fact, WEIRD parents report that collaborative engagement with their own children is far more likely to occur through parent-child play than in household chores; the reverse is true for samples of Indian and Peruvian villagers (Callaghan et al., 2011).

4.2 Extinguishing the Drive to Be Helpful

Harriet Rheingold, whose classic study established the apparently inherited proclivity for helping that emerges in early childhood, also interviewed parents of her subjects. These results are less well known. She found that WEIRD parents were not particularly appreciative of helpful toddlers: "To avoid what they viewed as interference they tried to accomplish the chores while the children were taking their naps" (Rheingold, 1982: 122). These findings were mirrored in an earlier interview study with mothers in the UK (Newson & Newson, 1976). Another study from the same era, in which mothers kept a log of all their four- and seven-year-olds' prosocial acts (including helping), found that the children averaged fewer than one such act per day (Grusec, 1991). More recent studies also find that WEIRD parents see their eager-to-help young children as unhelpful (Hammond, 2014). And even when WEIRD parents provide opportunities to helpful children or encourage them to do chores, their primary motivation may be the child's socialization or "character build-ing" rather than distributing the domestic labor over the whole family (Grusec, 1981). Somewhat older (e.g., 6+) children may be assigned chores on a contractual basis whereby suggesting or asking the child to help with activity not included in this understanding would be considered "unfair" (Coppens et al., 2018: 12), requiring additional compensation (e.g., "overtime").

Other obstacles might arise because of the complexity and opacity of modern domestic tools and equipment. WEIRD children may have a more difficult time learning to use a washing machine or food processor or vacuum cleaner than their village counterparts who can learn from observing and imitating the more trans-parent actions of collecting, planting, campfire cooking, wood chopping, and sweeping with a broom: "[T]he material environment offers no mechanical com-plexities such as elaborate machines, beyond the comprehension of the child. . . . The simple mechanical principles upon which a Manus (PNG) native builds and navigates his canoes, or builds his house, present no mysteries" (Mead, 1967: 235).

Then, too, a prominent characteristic of WEIRD child-rearing philosophy is "overprotectiveness" (Skenazy, 2009; Lancy, 2017a). A significant portion of a modern household toolkit would be deemed either threatening to the child or vulnerable to clumsy handling by the child. While WEIRD children may, on occasion, be asked to "hand mommy that spoon," they are not generally engaged deeply enough in the task to be able to, eventually, take it over.

Aside from outright denial of the child's offer to assist, another apparently common response is to transform the task at hand into a series of lessons (Gauvain, 2001; Morelli, Rogoff, & Angelillo 2003; Callaghan et al., 2011). For example, in a lab setting, WEIRD mothers were asked to invite their four-year-olds to participate in making some "crispy treats." From the outset, mothers treated the cooking project as a means to an end, rather than the end itself. It was not about shared work but affording the mothers teaching opportunities. WEIRD mothers created lessons that involved the science of cooking, the sensation of taste, and basic nutrition information. But most often they used the cooking activity as an occasion for enhancing children's literacy and basic mathematical skills. And while the study's authors valorize this behavior, they acknowledge that "a possible detrimental effect of an overly didactic parental focus during the cooking activity is that children may find the joint activity less fun or engaging" (Finn & Vandermaas-Peeler, 2013: unpaged). In the penultimate section of this Element, I discuss the myriad ways in which children learn through work – largely obviating the need to instruct them. In WEIRD society, this relationship is reversed as illustrated in a popular article titled "How to use laundry to teach kids learning skills." The author urges mothers to invite toddlers to help with the laundry because it provides a plethora of potential lessons: "Who knew that laundry offers the chance to teach kids their colors, textures, counting, size, matching skills, shapes and even expand their imaginations?" (Leverette, 2019).

An obvious consequence of the continued denial or deflection of helping overtures by toddlers is that the evident drive is extinguished – victim of "a childrearing philosophy focused heavily on pedagogy" (Callaghan et al., 2011: 109).[7] Consequently, older children rarely volunteer and frequently resist requests to help. The following is from a long-term, video-recorded ethnographic study of typical WEIRD families in the United States:

> In a study of 30 families in Los Angeles, "no child routinely assumed
> responsibility for household tasks without being asked . . . the overall picture

---

[7] The !Kung were cited earlier as an outlier where children are not expected or encouraged to assist with work, child care, and so on. Draper notes: "I never observed a man who was working . . . attempt to get help from his own or another child" (Draper, 1976: 212). Not surprisingly, "I can relate an incident in which Kxau was trying to get his youngest son, Kashe, to bring him something from the other side of camp. . . . Kxau repeatedly shouted to his son to bring him his tobacco from inside the family hut. The boy ignored his father's shouts, though !Kung camps are small, and the boy clearly could hear his father. Finally, Kxau bellowed out his command, glaring across at his son and the other youngsters sitting there. Kashe looked up briefly and yelled back, "Do it yourself, old man." A few minutes later Kxau did do it himself" (Draper, 1975: 92).

was one of effortful appeals by parents for help [who often] backtracked and did the task themselves ... [becoming, in effect] a valet for the child." (Ochs & Izquierdo, 2009: 399–400)

The following is drawn from an interview study contrasting the views of village (where children are routinely helpful) and cosmopolitan urban (Guadalajara) mothers:

[A] mother reported: "I'll walk into the bathroom and everything is all soapy, and she says to me 'I'm just cleaning.' I tell her, 'You know what? It's better that you don't clean anything for me, because I'm going to slip and fall in here.'" Mothers in the cosmopolitan community did not allow their children to take care of younger siblings, stating that childcare is the parent's responsibility alone, not the child's. One mother reported: "I tell her, 'Don't take roles that are not yours,' I tell her, 'Enjoy your childhood, you will be a mom one day.'" (Alcalá et al., 2014: 102, 104–5)

In WEIRD society, children no longer can be relied upon to manage and care for "their stuff," let alone take on a portion of the parent's chores:

"Mrs. York is trying to sort out the pieces of two games that have gotten mixed together. She tries again to get Jennifer to do her part [but] Jennifer complains [and] adds a dig at her mother, 'I always have to do stuff by myself and you just sit around.' Jennifer drags her feet ... whines ... complains ... about her mother [who argues and negotiates with her daughter]." (Miller & Cho, 2018:122)

These three studies are representative of a wave of similar field studies of WEIRD families around the globe.[8] A sampling from these accounts appears in Table 4.1.

In all these cases, parents likely deflected or rejected offers of assistance from toddlers, only to find that older children (from age six through the teen years), when requested to help, refused, did a slap-dash job, complied but with much whining and complaining, or bargained for payment or privileges.

Even within the global WEIRD culture, variability is to be expected in the degree to which child helpers are accommodated. In a comparative study, middle-class eighteen-month-old children and their mothers from Münster and Delhi were observed. Delhi mothers provided more "openings" for the child to be helpful, less praise for helping, and more admonishment for not helping: "Delhi toddlers helped more than Münster toddlers" (Giner Torréns & Kärtner, 2017: 353; see also Kärtner 2018). Even cosmopolitan Indian parents

---

[8] An internet survey of 500 US primarily middle-class families contradicts these studies in finding that parents reported their children took on more chores as they got older (Hammond & Brownell, 2018).

Table 4.1 Unhelpful children in WEIRD societies

In West Berlin "parents alone are responsible for . . . the reproduction of daily life . . . the child is the recipient of care and services" (Zeiher, 2001: 43).

In a case study from Los Angeles, a parent spends a lot of time cajoling/guiding a five-year-old into making her bed. It becomes a big dramatic production after she initially refuses, claiming incompetence. In a comparative case from Rome, the father does not even bother trying to get his eight-year-old daughter to make her bed, he does it himself, while complaining that her large collection of stuffed animals and her decision to move to the top bunk make his task much harder (Fasulo, et al., 2007: 16–18).

Genevan children "use the vociferous defeat strategy. They comply with what is asked of them but . . . cry, scream, bang doors, lock themselves up in their rooms to sulk and so on. . . . Some . . . agree to submit if their parents can prove their demands are well-founded" (Montandon, 2001: 62).

A lengthy description of "'shepherding' a four-year-old Swedish child to bed at night shows this as a major undertaking [consuming] the mother's time and energy" (Cekaite, 2010: 17–19).

In Norway, children's "contribution to the household is paid for by the parents [which indicates] that housework remains the responsibility of the parent" (Nilsen & Wærdahl, 2014: 3).

In the Marshall Islands (Micronesia), drastic culture change has profoundly affected the role of children in the family economy: "Adults do say that children today are different. . . . 'The children of the past knew how to work. Children today, they don't know how to work. They just play . . . [they] are very naughty'" (Berman, 2019: 151).

In the modern Australian middle/upper class, children no longer work. When queried, children treat "the term *work* as having one meaning only: waged work outside the home. Work is something that one 'goes to' and that is done in exchange for money" (Bowes & Goodnow, 1996: 302).

Fast forward twenty years and many WEIRD families use a smartphone app to remind and guide children in doing chores while keeping track of how much they are owed by parents (Coppens & Alcala, 2015: 99).

expect children to be helpful and convey that expectation quite deliberately. Child caretakers in modern Gaberone, Botswana expressed parallel views (Marea Tsamaase, personal communication, June 18, 2019; see also Tudge, 2008: 169). German parents might like children to be helpful but treat it as a completely learned behavior – praiseworthy if displayed, needing cultivation if not. In fact, when German mothers attempt to promote helping in their toddlers, they do so aggressively through coaxing, instructing, and rewarding, acting as if the child had no inherent motivation to be helpful (Köster et al., 2016). As noted earlier, praise and rewards actually *suppress* helping, and the aggressive scaffolding of German mothers may be counterproductive (Giner Torréns & Kärtner, 2017).

In the United States, parents lavishly praise children – not necessarily because they need and value their help but to build up the child's self-esteem and sense of self-worth (Miller & Cho, 2018). It appears that many WEIRD parents unwittingly extinguish the helping instinct in their toddlers. One very WEIRD result of this trend is the increasing appearance of "adulting" classes – at least in the United States. Adulting classes are aimed at those in their twenties and early thirties who have never learned domestic skills like infant and child care, cooking, sewing, home maintenance, and so on. Students in these classes tell similar tales:

> Elena Toumaras, 29, is currently learning an adult skill she was never *taught* before – cooking. Toumaras is attending a cooking class in Queens to help fill a gap in her life skill knowledge. "I was so used to, when living at home, my mom always cooking," she said. "Doing simple things now that I'm on my own, I'm struggling with it." Elena says she's finally learning skills she's sorry she wasn't *taught* years ago. (O'Kane, 2018, italics added)

The clear implication here is that WEIRD children who are not expected to assist or collaborate with others in doing family chores fail to learn necessary life skills. Domestic tasks are all practiced exclusively by adults who, in the interest of efficiency, "fail" to "teach" their children – leading to the need for adulting classes.

4.3 The End of the Helper Stage

From both lab studies and the ethnographic record, we can deduce that the helper stage begins around fourteen months. Unfortunately, to date, the lab studies have extended only to about thirty to thirty-six months, so they do not provide a clear end point. However, as just noted, numerous ethnographic studies across a range of WEIRD societies indicate that, in the absence of careful cultivation, WEIRD kids may become quite resistant to appeals for help by as early as age six. Hence, the helper stage is truncated by the explicit rejection of the toddler's offers of assistance. Elsewhere, the stage ends as the helper becomes a worker (Grove & Lancy, 2015; Lancy, 2018).

This latter process can be demonstrated in a predictable – and increasingly rare – context, namely the family farm. In a survey of Wisconsin (USA) dairy farm families, preschoolers pitched in to help, but by age seven, all children were assigned daily chores: a seven-year-old feeds the calves, an eleven-year-old drives the tractor, and a twelve-year-old milks the cows. Older children were also responsible for various domestic chores including sib-care (Zepeda & Kim, 2006).

In the context of an agrarian society, helping – which is welcomed and supported – gradually evolves into working. Unlike the helper, a worker is fully competent at assigned chores and can work solo without supervision. The worker is reliable and does not wander off to play before completing the chore (Lancy, 2018) – as a young Mazahua (Mexico) child helper might, for example, "walk 'in and out' of adult activities, tak[ing] up tasks and leav[ing] them again" (de Haan, 1999: 78). The child who has left the helper stage is expected to take the initiative and self-assign chores, especially with respect to taking care of their own needs. For example, Otgono, a six-year-old Mongol boy, "took the initiative to stir tea with a ladle. ... On laundry day, he happily hand-washed small items. When ... his trousers got torn he took a needle and thread from Tuyaa's sewing box and mended them" (Michelet, 2016: 233).

A surprising number of societies mark a milestone in the juvenile's life course that has significant implications for the transition from helper to worker. The Kpelle (Liberia) refer to this event or period as "getting sense" (Lancy, 1996: 118), where sense encompasses a broad interpretation of *intelligence* (Gardner, 1983). For the Bakkarwal (nomadic pastoralists in Jammu and Kashmir), "*Osh* comes to a human child increasingly from the age of seven or eight years [and] it is *osh* which enables a shepherd to tend his flocks well, day and night" (Rao, 1998: 59). Among the Inuit (Arctic), the acquisition of *isuma* signals the child's readiness to tackle a range of essential tasks on a routine basis, often without prompting:

> *Isuma* refers to consciousness, thought, reason, memory, will – to cerebral processes in general – and the possession of *isuma* is a major criterion of maturity. Saying that a person has *isuma* is equivalent to saying that she or he exercises good judgment, reason, and emotional control at all times, in addition to the skills appropriate to his or her age, gender, and role. (Briggs, 1991: 267)

Isuma can be a descriptor of the child's arrival at a distinct transition or stage in the life course, but it may also be signaled by a more specific event:

> For a boy from the Copper Eskimo, an important transitional event was the ceremony accompanying the first kill. When the first seal was killed and pulled from its breathing hole, it was dragged over the body of the successful young hunter. The seal was then apportioned by a close relative (usually an

uncle) and given to the predetermined seal-sharing partnership. (Damas, 2011: 42)

In a rural village in NE Brazil, "a child, upon reaching the age of eight, would receive the present of a hoe from his father. The hoe given to a child of this age was special for being smaller and lighter than one used by an adult. Such hoes were not fashioned specially for children, they were simply old ones worn down from years of use by adults. . . . The receiving of one's first hoe in this way [is] a rite of passage. . . . The day following its presentation, the child would be expected to leave for the field along with all the other working members of the family. (Mayblin, 2010: 34–35)

"!Kung boys at around twelve are given a fine bow and arrows by their father to improve their prospects" (Shòstak, 1981: 83). When Hadza boys "are considered responsible enough, they are finally permitted to use poisoned arrows." (Blurton Jones & Marlowe, 2002: 217)

The juvenile worker becomes a kind of cog in the domestic economy. Earlier, the juvenile may have taken on relatively undemanding tasks, such as child care or fetching firewood, but now their increased strength and skill permit them to undertake tasks that would otherwise fall to adolescents or adults. In middle childhood, the juvenile makes a critical contribution to the household but still depends heavily on others for food and other critical resources (Kramer, 2011: 538):

[A] Pumé boy living on the llanos of Venezuela might be successful in catching enough fish to feed himself, his siblings and parents, but is dependent on shares of processed plant food and hunted game from others. A Pumé girl might be able to weave a burden basket but is not strong enough to collect the moriche palm fronds or strip and process the fiber. (Kramer, 2011: 535)

Because of international child labor laws, children may be particularly needy in terms of ready cash to pay for clothing, school fees, and the like.

While a helper might choose whom to assist and/or what activity to get involved in, a child worker is assigned particular responsibilities commensurate with their strength and skill, the job inventory, and the makeup of the domestic labor force: "Tsimané (Bolivia) parents expect their children to be more fully engaged in productive work, gaining individual responsibility in activities like fruit gathering, help in the agricultural fields, and taking care of animals" (Martínez-Rodríguez, 2009: 65). Parents are charged with the responsibility of providing assignments or chores that facilitate the helper-worker transition.

Of course, some juveniles may require a bit of prodding to stay "up to the mark." A Sebei (Uganda) mother condemns a "lazy" daughter by saying, "I hope that you have stomach pains and dysentery" (Goldschmidt, 1976: 259). A Gusii (Kenya) child who fails to carry out a chore may be ordered out of the house and implicitly refused food and shelter (LeVine & LeVine, 1963). A Kwoma (PNG) child is rewarded for industry but also scolded, beaten, hazed by peers, and denied food for any sign of laxity (Whiting, 1941). Chuuk Island (Micronesia) children may be caned in addition to being denied food (Gladwin & Sarason, 1953). An Amhara (Ethiopia) adult may hasten a child to their chores "by throwing clods of dirt or manure at him" (Levine, 1965: 266): "Folk stories, involving *peranti* (lazy) characters who suffer dire consequences for their behavior, are told purposely to indicate disapproval and instill a sense of fear and shame in children who require reminders of the tenets of Matsigenka (Peru) collaboration" (Ochs & Izquierdo, 2009: 395–6). These examples and others (Lancy, 2018) reinforce the argument that unprompted helping may become attenuated at the end of the helper stage. The continued imperative that juveniles feel to be helpful must be scaffolded by their culture and, occasionally, the scaffolding may include ridicule and punishment.

Across the ethnographic record, the transition from helper to worker tends to occur earlier in agrarian societies, particularly among pastoralists. But the age range from six to ten years seems to encompass the transition period across all modes of production, and this range corresponds, not coincidentally, to the period of middle childhood. Studies show that this is the stage where physiological and cognitive changes occur that are associated with growing physical, social, and intellectual maturity (Rogoff et al., 1975; Lancy & Grove, 2011). If fourteen months marks the onset of the helper stage – corresponding to early childhood – then I would argue that the end of the helper stage corresponds to the onset of middle childhood.

Schooling is an evident impediment to a juvenile's transition from the helper stage to the status of worker. Across the world in poorer communities, schooling may be treated as an unaffordable luxury – especially for girls, whose assigned workload may be higher than boys' (Hollos & Leis, 1989). In many communities studied by anthropologists, school attendance tends to decline as the child's value as a worker increases: "It is difficult to say precisely when [Ghanaian] children become net economic assets to their families, but education delay[s] that transition" (Lord, 2011: 102).

In WEIRD society, the notion that schooling (and, increasingly, extracurricular activities like music performance, dance, and sports) represents the child's *work* is widespread, as reflected in terms like "Good Job!" applied to homework, schoolwork, and seatwork. However, this view is driven not only by the incompatibility of school and work but also in a child-centered society (amounting to a "neontocracy," cf. Lancy, 2015b), children occupy a privileged position. Real work by children is practically taboo in WEIRD families. Taken broadly, work is something only adults do. Adolescent employment, even casual summer jobs (flipping burgers at McDonald's, lifeguarding at the pool) has declined steadily (DeSilver, 2019).

Referring again to children growing up on farms, Zepeda and Kim (2006) found that families were careful to ensure that both chores and academic study received their due. This pattern, which today is exceptional, was the norm in the past century. In Laurence Wylie's ethnography of a farming village in France in the mid-twentieth century, children's only opportunity to play occurred on the walk home from school, as all but the very youngest had chores (Wylie, 1957: 69). Earlier in US history, this rapprochement between helping and schooling had not yet emerged: "German settlers in Pennsylvania opposed education on the ground that it would make children lazy and dissatisfied with farm work" (MacElroy, 1917: 59). In contemporary rural villages as well, there is evident conflict: "Inuit children who previously spent their days helping parents with hunting, trapping, fishing, skin preparation, and general household chores now spend much of the day in an institutional setting, learning skills unrelated, and sometimes antithetical, to those emphasized at home" (Condon, 1987: 157).

Globally, the growth of formal education has inexorably reduced or eliminated children's participation in the domestic economy. Rogoff and colleagues were able to track this change over a sixty-year timespan in San Pedro, a Mayan community in Guatemala. Aside from changes in children's activity, their patterns of learning also changed dramatically: "The limited opportunities to observe and be involved in ongoing activities may increase the likelihood that children depend on others to organize their attention, motivation, and learning of the information and skills required in maturity, as in schools" (Rogoff, Correa-Chávez, & Cotuc, 2005: 227).

The helper stage is preparatory to a future as a skilled and responsible worker. In the next section, I will review two of the underlying processes that are inherent to the helper stage: learning to collaborate and learning practical skills. I will also show how these affordances of the helper stage are of much less value in a society dominated by teaching as the primary mode of enculturation.

5 What Are the Benefits of the Child's Need to Help?

The helper stage is a period in which the juvenile's nascent motivation and readiness to contribute to the domestic economy first appears. In most societies, this motivation is nurtured and guided by those older than the would-be helper. In Section 1, I cited Kramer's (2011) argument that kin, mothers especially, have a strong motive for enabling the child helper, insofar as the helpful child relieves others of some of their burdens, permitting them to invest their time in ways that expand the family and thereby enhance genetic fitness. In Section 2, I argued that the juvenile, from at least fourteen months and perhaps earlier, is primed by nature with the need to be helpful. The payoff for these overtures (which may be rebuffed) would be the opportunity to win the attention and approbation of the immediate family and, ultimately, the larger community. The barrier to such affiliation may be higher in some societies than others, but obstacles to affiliation typically lead to greater efforts to offer credible assistance.

I want to return to the issue of benefits here to identify two further benefits to both helpers and the helped, to be discussed shortly. Usually, benefits offset costs. An important cost has already been touched on, namely, in accommodating the would-be helper, the potential recipient of aid may compromise their own efficiency as well as the value of the goods being procured or manufactured. A second significant cost involves possible injury to the child. Targets of assistance include butchering sites where sharp instruments are wielded; cooking sites with open fires and scalding hot cooking vessels; bush foraging, which places potentially harmful plants, insects, reptiles, and predators in the child's path; and hunting excursions, where the child might be in the line of fire or exposed to the deadly toxins used to coat arrow tips. Not only is the child helper at risk in such scenarios but as child-minders, they also may place their charges at risk (Paradise, 1987).

From an evolutionary perspective, these evident costs reinforce the view that there must be distinct and significant benefits associated with child helpers. Two of the primary benefits will be discussed in the following subsections: learning to work collaboratively and learning valued skills as a novice member of a working party.

5.1 Affiliation Earned through Collaboration

According to de Waal, humans are born with a drive to "fit in" or the "desire to be like others" (2001: 230). Tomasello claims that children "are sensitive from a young age to their own interdependence with others in collaborative activities ... and they value conformity to the group as a marker of group identity" (2009: 45–6). Children as young as seventeen months demonstrate IGF=*Ingroup Favoritism*: "an evolved adaptation [that] serves to maintain the individual's reputation as a reliable collaborator ... and decreases the risk for exclusion from the group" (Jin & Baillargeon, 2017: 8200). Combine these claims with the ubiquity of "toddler rejection" discussed in Section 2 and the fact that, in most societies, children earn social capital through being helpful, and you have a suite of evolutionarily significant benefits for the helper. Helping serves to cement the child's social affiliation and social standing. That is, voluntary offers of assistance by children appear to be both welcome and appreciated, and the absence of same may be cause for concern about the child's character. But because open praise is usually frowned on, these positive feelings may be hard for a participant observer to detect.

Helping may well serve as a necessary precursor to the extremely important ability to collaborate with others. As Tomasello and Vaish note:

> [H]umans procure the vast majority of their food through collaborative efforts of one type or another ... [and] there is evidence that children help more in a collaborative context than a non-collaborative context ... [leading to a claim that there is] a fundamental human drive to collaborate with others to achieve joint and shared goals. (2013: 238–9, 242).

Pygmy foragers, who depend on net hunting, provide an excellent illustration of this vital collaboration and children's participation. A net is strung across a promising stretch of forest; "beaters," starting at a certain distance from the net, drive small mammals, such as duiker, into the net where they are clubbed to death. Later, the catch is butchered to ease transport back to camp. Men, women, and children participate: as a group, they can obtain more food than individuals hunting singly (which men do). Children who are old enough to keep up with the hunters as they travel to the site are given one or more responsibilities, including setting up and holding the net, beating, preventing animals from escaping the net and helping carry the return load. Children make other contributions on the hunt:

> Walking through the forest, men, women, and children ... frequently check tree hollows and burrows for small prey and tree trunks for signs of lizards. ...
> All net-hunt participants, but especially women and children, opportunistically gather insects, fruit, nuts, and plants whenever they are encountered. (Lupo & Schmitt, 2002)

Agriculture typically provides numerous settings where a mixed-age working party can be accommodated. Tapajós River (Brazil) communities depend on manioc as a staple. The plant is cultivated, harvested, peeled of its fibrous skin, sun dried, chopped, crushed, and sifted into flour. The flour is then toasted in an oven before being turned into dough and, for a portion, sold. Medaets (2011) describes a varied cast of individuals, ranging in age from two to seventy, and settings in which all this family activity is carried out. Everyone is involved: Ranilson (fifteen) weeds the manioc plants; Luis (nine), Anderson (six), and Zilane (four) apply pressure to the pole used in pressing the dough; Everton (eight) washes up; everyone gathers firewood, but only Henrique (ten) starts the fire. While João (thirty-five) is in charge of roasting, his son Elder (seventeen) stirs the flour in the oven. Zilma (six) assists her grandmother in squeezing *cupuaçu* juice for everyone's refreshment. As the toasting oven is at a distant village, add two hours of casual foraging in each direction for the convivial work party.

With modernization, new venues are created, and children are eager participants. Several accounts provide descriptions of the process whereby Mazahua child helpers become collaborators in constructing a market stall:

> Role switching between observer-performer, as well as between marginal and central performer, permitted children to gradually gain more expertise while being fully involved and sharing responsibility for the activity. It is the "being close" to the expert in a "same identity" role (instead of being a student), which probably explains the ... effectiveness of this way of "organizing learning." ... When an older, more experienced child took over a tricky part of the process, the less experienced child observed closely with what appeared to be a clear intent to better grasp how to do it. Once the more difficult part was accomplished, and the less experienced child was able to successfully carry out the next step in the process, he or she took over eagerly while the more experienced child watched, ready to correct or help when necessary. ... This kind of reciprocity in favor of a collective effort ... appears to reflect a social orientation growing out of an awareness of belonging to, participating in, and being part of a social entity. (Paradise & de Haan, 2009: 196)

There is more to helping than the willingness and ability to carry out a series of isolated chores or helping a single individual with a single problem – the default paradigm for the lab studies reviewed earlier. In the societies studied by anthropologists, helpers inevitably become collaborators, and facility as a collaborator is tantamount in these societies to facility as an adult member of society. Failure to effectively collaborate would be an enormous liability.

Barbara Rogoff and colleagues have carried out many cross-cultural comparisons of collaboration by Mexican indigenous children – valuable and steadfast helpers (Paradise & Rogoff, 2009) – versus children from more cosmopolitan backgrounds. Just as helping by children appears to either flourish or perish depending on the degree of welcome afforded helpers, so too is collaboration affected by supportive versus non-supportive environments (Rogoff et al., 2017). Indigenous or "heritage" communities sustain an especially sophisticated form of collaboration in which children learn to be "attentive to each other's efforts, flexibly adjust their own actions to align with the direction of the group and take initiative when they see what needs to be done and support others in doing the same" (Rogoff et al., 2017: 880).

In a task that called for collaboration, a trio of five- to fifteen-year-old Mexican heritage siblings worked together, completing the task smoothly with little discussion or direction (López et al., 2012). WEIRD children, by contrast, tended to divvy up the task so each could work alone. And there was much conflict and argument regarding turn taking. This study has been replicated with two or three children in various settings with varied problems to solve, and the results are consistent (Mejía-Arauz et al., 2007; Correa-Chávez, 2016; Alcalá, Rogoff, & Frairea, 2018).

Correa-Chávez (2016: 130) reported that Mexican sibling pairs, age six to eleven, were video recorded as they assembled a three-dimensional puzzle, guided only by the presence of a completed example. The sample children from a rural village, with little history of schooling, collaborated readily and effectively, with little or no verbal exchange, whereas the sample drawn from a middle-class, "high-schooling" community tended to work alone, communicated verbally, and drifted off task.

Other important conclusions from this line of research include the finding that the child as helper phenomenon "travels" from rural Mexican communities. Immigrants to the United States expect their children to participate in collaborative work as well as carry out routine chores (Orellana, 2001). Aside from ethnicity, Los Angeles families where mothers had less than a ninth-grade education held high expectations for their children as helpers, and those with higher levels of schooling held very low expectations (Klein, Graesch, & Izquierdo, 2009).

Children who work collaboratively are also able to apply their collaborative skills to the novel, more school-like settings used in the experiments just discussed. WEIRD children, by contrast, who do not participate as helpers in collaborative household activity, cannot collaborate effectively in the experimental tasks. Usually one member of the dyad takes charge, or the two take turns. And in this era of high-stakes testing, classrooms present few opportunities to learn to work collaboratively (de Haan 2018).

López et al. (2012: 873) cite an earlier field study by Susan Phillips (1983), who found that Warm Springs Indian students in Oregon, when asked to work on group projects, worked together effectively without intervention from the teacher, whereas Anglo students in the school often disputed over turns, who would lead, and how to carry out the tasks – requiring teacher intervention. Clearly, the Indian children brought to school the collaborative strategies that were in demand in their community. The Anglo students had been shaped by the WEIRD child-rearing philosophy dedicated to child individualism (Kärtner et al., 2010). Miller and Cho's (2018) recent work provides many illustrations of the promotion of individualism over collaboration:

> [P]arents are urged to honor the child's perspective: "Treat your child as
> a separate, independent person with the right to his own feelings, ideas, and
> attitudes. Appreciate and recognize what he *can* do – no matter how small the

triumph" (Miller & Cho 2018: 137). . . . *[T]hey'll have the confidence to do their own thing and not be led by other people*" (Miller & Cho, 2018: 69, italics added).

Meanwhile, there is a growing recognition that like "adulting" (see p. 43), children's inability to collaborate is a deficiency that must be remedied by – teaching (Sparks, 2017)!

I am arguing that the spontaneous emergence of helping is an essential prerequisite to becoming a skilled collaborator. And the human ability to collaborate in a wide variety of enterprises, including childcare, has been credited with the success of our species.

5.2 Collaboration Leads to Learning

Another clear benefit of the compunction to pitch in and be helpful is that it is through helping and, by extension, collaboration that children learn their culture. Across the ethnographic record and in the annals of history, learning through doing is the norm; deliberate instruction is a rare event. Teaching is expensive from a fitness perspective because a mature, highly productive individual has to reduce their output to take on the role of instructor (Lancy 2016b). A far more efficient approach is to take advantage of the child's willingness to pitch in and get involved in a helpful fashion, which leads, inevitably, to incidental learning.

As demonstrated so convincingly by Rogoff and colleagues (Rogoff, 2003; Correa-Chávez, Mejía-Arauz, & Rogoff, 2015) over numerous studies covering decades, children must become involved as participants to fully experience the tasks of interest. They can closely observe competent models, and they can work their way up from very simple sub-tasks to more complex components. If they hope to receive any guidance at all from an expert, they must place themselves in close proximity, show they are attending, and better yet be willing to assist where needed (Paradise & Rogoff, 2009). Offering to help out can be seen as the "price of admission." Each of the anecdotes in Table 5.1 illustrates culturally patterned learning through participation.

If children want to learn practical skills, and they clearly do, their primary option is to "learn on the job," and, as expressed by Mesoudi, "Children seem to be predisposed to rapidly and automatically acquire huge amounts of information from other people. They are, in a sense, 'cultural sponges,' soaking up knowledge from those around them" (2011: 15).

Learning through collaboration encompasses the gamut of skills, practical and social, that are expected of mature individuals. Many have argued, for example, that infant care and childcare are learned largely through serving as an alloparent to one's younger siblings (Veile & Kramer, 2018). Girls are drawn to

Table 5.1 Children learning through collaborative activity

"Miskito (Honduras) [children] learn about fish and fishing strategies via observations [and] experience as participants on fishing trips. . . . They are frequently brought on excursions in dugout canoes with older relatives who fish. As youngsters, children often contribute by gathering and managing the fish caught by family members. [Consequently] they exhibit high levels of knowledge relatively early in life" (Koster, Bruno, & Burns, 2016: 114, 117).

Touareg (Niger) boys and girls spend several years as assistants to older siblings, learning the different kinds of forage, the idiosyncrasies of each animal and which ones need extra vigilance. He or she gradually takes on more responsibility until, at age ten, the young herder solos (Spittler, 1998).

Tsimané children "learn" the basic geography of their forest and riverine environment by tagging along as helpers to adults and older siblings during numerous hunting and foraging expeditions (Davis & Cashdan, 2020).

"During this period there is no formal training [among the Mbuti Pygmies (Congo)], but boys and girls alike learn all there is to be learned by simple emulation and by assisting their parents and elders in various tasks" (Turnbull, 1965: 179).

"In Samoa, a child may dig up worms and donate them to a fisher in hopes of being invited along to observe the [fishing] process" (Odden, 2007: 219).

"A [Nahua] 30-year-old woman explained, remembering back to when she was 5: 'We listen to how things are and we also watch; then one day they call on us to start participating.' As children grow, the parents' request to carry out the activity fades away. An 8-year-old boy explained: 'My mother didn't have to be running after us, because we knew we were supposed to do it. It was my role to tend the sheep together with my little brother; we were expected to do it'" (Fernández 2015: 64).

" [A] BaYaka mother cutting koko leaves into thin strips, a task which requires fine motor skills, sometimes did so alongside her five-year-old daughter, herself also cutting koko, though with less success. Among the Hadza, a young child waiting while her mother dug tubers sometimes assisted her mother or dug in an adjacent hole with a smaller digging stick, whether or not the hole actually yielded a tuber" (Lew-Levy et al., 2019: 314).

Apache [N. America] "youths [might] accompany a large hunting trip. They fetch wood and water for the camp and look after the horses, at the same time gaining experience by being with skilled hunters . . . learning much of what they ultimately would know about hunting from observation without direct instruction" (Goodwin & Goodwin, 1942: 475).

"Tsimané (Bolivia) girls are expected to perform household tasks and accompany mothers and other relatives to agricultural fields. Such close interaction could facilitate the transmission of ethnobotanical knowledge and

Table 5.1 (cont.)

skills from the older to the younger generation" (Reyes-García et al., 2009: 283).

"The first principle of Ojibwa (North America) learning is a preference for experiential knowledge. Indigenous pedagogy values a person's ability to learn by observing, listening, and participating with a minimum of intervention or instruction. This pattern of direct learning by seeing and doing, without asking questions, makes Ojibwa children diverse learners. They do not have a single homogenous learning style" (Battiste, 2002: 15).

Canoe making for the Khanty (Siberia) is a complex process. The challenge is in wetting, heating, and bending the wood to open the timber wide enough to accommodate the spreaders or thwarts without cracking. The goal is a small, sturdy and lightweight vessel. Canoe makers learn through "watching, assisting . . . and then by trying for themselves" (Jordan, 2014: 252).

"Maya children's motivation to contribute seemed pivotal in their . . . acquisition of medicinal plant knowledge" (Jiménez-Balam, Alcalá, & Salgado, 2019: 1).

babies and tend to hover in close proximity to women with infants, eager to volunteer their services. Initially, they might do no more than hold the infant, but the alloparent role will grow in complexity and time allocated as they learn – under the loose guidance of the infant's mother and other senior women. In WEIRD society, an avalanche of infant care books, videos, blogs, and infant-care classes attest to the disappearance of sib-care (and "babysitting" as well, cf. Forman-Brunell, 2009) and the learning opportunities it provided.

While sib-care may be universal or nearly so, learning via collaboration involves different activities and skills, depending on the nature of the work. Koster, Bruno, and Burns (2016) carried out a study of "ethnobiological knowledge" of Mayangna and Miskito (Nicaragua) villagers across a wide age range. They were testing the assumption that "individuals continue to accumulate ethnobiological knowledge throughout their lives, resulting in greater expertise among the elder generations" (Koster et al., 2016: 113). They measured various attributes of fishing skill and knowledge of fish behavior and ecology. Skill and knowledge did not develop in a linear fashion with age. Rather, it was driven by the individual's investment in fishing and in observing and interacting with knowledgeable fishers. This suggests again that children learn through collaborating, observing, listening, and practicing and can, thereby, reach a high level of proficiency while still young.

Parallel results were obtained in a study of botanical knowledge on Dominica Island in the Caribbean. Children's knowledge of plants was positively affected

Figure 5.1 Caring for the baby (Mali: Barbara Polak)

by living in a multi-family, versus single-family, compound and by the presence of a greater number of siblings in the household. This suggests that when children have more opportunities to interact collaboratively with others, their knowledge base grows more rapidly (Quinlan et al., 2016).

This drive to collaborate is typically enacted in social environments that are extremely supportive and child friendly. Here is a description of collaboration among Batek (Borneo) hunters and gatherers:

> Trips to the forest are often festive occasions especially when the group is rather large . . . the Batek . . . adjust their speed of walking to the level of the least competent member of the group. . . . Aside from the explicit details of locations, conditions, and accessibility, verbalized information might include narratives and tall tales recounting the day's experiences or memories of past adventures. These are shared usually after work or at night thus providing an excellent context for children and young people to learn second-hand through the errors of the adults. . . . For children, these are their everyday classrooms. . . . Children also bring knowledge back to the parents. For example, children roaming free in the forest will spot much that is new and significant . . . and will inform the parents and other adults. In one case, a mother was complaining about local scarcity of *takop* "wild tubers"; her son pointed out to her a vine that he had seen, and this knowledge was acted upon. . . . [C]hildren, even at this age, are considered to be equal partners in the conversation." (Lye, 1997: 70, 101, 108–9, 351)

Note that it is not just children who learn through collaborative activity; adolescents and adults usually prefer group work, which affords ample opportunity to learn informally from peers (Koster et al., 2016) without the need for the social hierarchy implied by teaching (Borofsky, 1987). Furthermore, working in a collaborative context provides "frequent opportunities to observe innovations, evaluate their success, and imitate traits judged most successful or most common" (Hill et al., 2011: 1288):

> [!Kung hunters] report at length and dramatically on excursions and hunts [as] people are gathered around the fire ... indirect adult communication of important information seems comparable to the indirect way that young men acquire information about animals and technology, which appears to be quite simply a matter of watching and listening to other people and then trying for oneself. There is almost no direct teaching. (Blurton Jones & Konner, 1976: 338–9)

Humans appear to be equipped with cognitive skills that are adapted to learning in these scenarios, and several of Warneken's (2015b) lab studies identify these skills. One such is children's ability to take in and process information from the environment indicating an unlearned capacity for what Gaskins and Paradise call "open attention" that can be deployed to good effect in social settings as well as in the natural environment (2010: 104). They describe open attention as wide angled and abiding. The first means that the individual is aware of and attends to a great deal of the environment at one time rather than attending to only one information source (video game, teacher). The second means that attention is sustained rather than episodic or short term (2010: 99–100). A recent experimental study compared isolated Himba forager/pastoralists with British subjects on tests of attention. Himba participants showed more efficient selective attention than did the Western participants (Caparos et al., 2013). This suggests that WEIRD society, with its emphasis on "pay attention to ... mommy, the teacher, the monitor, the lecture," leads to an attenuation of these native information-gathering skills.

Ingold neatly summarizes the contrast between indigenous and WEIRD models of pedagogy, illustrating the self-initiated and collaborative basis for the former: "In the passage of human generations, each one contributes to the knowledgeability of the next, not by handing down a corpus of disembodied, context-free information, but by setting up, through their activities, the environmental contexts within which successors develop their own ... skills" (Ingold, 2001: 142). As noted throughout this Element, WEIRD society does not nurture learning via helping and collaborating. There is, rather, the tendency to firmly define the roles of adults and children as teachers/pupils (de Haan,

2001). WEIRD children develop an expectation that learning occurs largely via teacher-organized lessons: "Teachers, as well as parents with extensive schooling themselves … closely manage young children's attention and discourage attention to surrounding events" (Silva, Shimpi, & Rogoff, 2015: 209). Several recent empirical studies affirm this contrast.

Children from traditional Mexican communities attended to a toy construction demonstration ostensibly directed to another child and yet learned enough from this observation to successfully complete the task. In contrast, "children from families with extensive schooling may rely more on having their attention directed by adults and muster less attention when no one is telling them to attend" (Silva, Correa-Chavéz, & Rogoff, 2011: 909). In a subsequent study, "a sample of primarily European-American children learned better from direct teaching situations, whereas Yucatec Mayan children learned just as well from observing others' interactions" (Silva et al., 2015: 209). A critical corollary to these findings has emerged from studies of speech directed at children. While WEIRD children are the target of a large volume of direct speech from birth, indigenous children are rarely spoken to directly, especially in a didactic mode (Cristia et al., 2017). Instead, children are expected to overhear or eavesdrop on conversations where they are third or passive parties (de León, 2011). Empirical studies have verified that children may learn as well from such indirect forms of communication as from directed speech (Akhtar 2005; D. E. Sperry, L. Sperry, & Miller, 2018).

I have characterized the helper stage as a *developmental niche* that, in supportive societies, nurtures the growth of prosocial behavior. As I have described, a number of other corollary benefits grow out of the helper stage: affiliation with the community, becoming an effective collaborator, and acquisition of the cultural toolkit of essential skills and values.

6 Summary and Conclusions

To fully understand and appreciate the significance of child helpers, it is necessary to reconsider a basic assumption about human development. It is widely acknowledged that there is a long juvenile period in human life history and that the juvenile is dependent on others for care and food. However, more recent field studies of child workers strongly suggest that juveniles act to reduce their dependency on others and assist in reducing the workload of those who provision them. Children frequently care for younger siblings, freeing up their mothers to spend time in food production. Child foragers and hunters not only provide food for themselves, but they also may share their found resources with others. By recasting childhood as a period of transition from total dependency (early infancy) and responsibility-free play to legitimate participation in the domestic economy, we can see the role a child helper stage might play.

The child helper stage begins in late infancy, and, with very few exceptions, children during this period eagerly volunteer to assist or pitch in. Because the helper, at this age, lacks the physical attributes, knowledge, and skills to be truly useful, they may be rebuffed or redirected. The high motivation is evident in the child's resilient and persistent attempts to fine-tune their assistance through observing and practicing relevant skills. They will be aided in finding suitable tasks within their capacity and, in fact, many common tasks, such as errand running, are designated for children of this age.

The child helper can be described as "on probation," a "novice," or an "intern," meaning they are not fully competent and are expected to learn by observing, imitating, and following the lead of those more competent. This status also carries with it the idea that the child is free to opt out of participation as they get tired, distracted, or bored. There is recognition of the limits imposed by immaturity and expectations are adjusted accordingly. The helper stage fits well the idea of a developmental niche, where maturational processes that are biological are complemented by cultural practices that scaffold and nurture the child's emergent abilities.

In seeking to understand the drive to be helpful, one persistent goad may be the toddler's low status and lack of consideration. Many societies display toddler rejection, whereby the no-longer-precious child is treated like an unwelcome burden and shunted off to be cared for by other, slightly older children. Denied the breast, forced to travel on their own power, they may be quite unhappy. But volunteering to help is often treated as a legitimate means of reattaching to one's mother and, more generally, feeds the need to affiliate with the group. Eventually, the child's growing competence and reliability lead to recognition as a full-fledged "member" or "person."

Although this Element is focused on helping, sharing is, obviously, complementary. In particular, children are often able to gather wild foods through foraging; through sharing their bounty, they can claim the same social capital they earn by helping others. In fact, many societies seem to value sharing over helping in that deliberate efforts are used to stimulate sharing behavior, whereas helping may be taken for granted.

The child helper stage begins in late infancy and represents the onset of a long period of development as a worker. The helper may become engaged with work either directly, through a successful bid to help or indirectly, through play. In playing with objects, children wield real, scaled-down or replica tools, and they can develop considerable skill through playful practice – guided by their observation of more mature tool users. In make-believe play, children act out the roles of child minder, house sweeper, food preparer, hunter, herd boy, *ad infinitum*. Play themes are solidly grounded in the local reality; fantasy is very rare. And they are not just practicing discrete skills, as they might in object play, but the social behaviors and speech elements associated with activities they might soon be involved in.

Although child helping is a recent subject of inquiry, our understanding of the phenomenon has advanced rapidly because of the rare congruence of two very different lines of research. First, the ethnographic record is replete with references to child helpers, and some of the earliest cross-cultural research on childhood tallied significant amounts of helping/working in the child's daily routine. The ethnographic record also reveals the processes whereby child helpers are woven into the domestic economy. Helping has also been the subject of a vigorous program of experimental lab research simulating a helping episode. These episodes pair an experimenter who experiences some difficulty and a child who is in a position to assist – if they choose to do so. Just as the ethnographic record shows child helpers to be ubiquitous, the lab research, with numerous replications, varied aged samples, varied conditions, and elaborate controls, also shows child helpers as a biological universal. The drive to be helpful appears early (by fourteen months); would-be helpers are not easily dissuaded or distracted; and their behavior is altruistic, not motivated by reward, approval, or expectation of future payback.

The proposal that there is a helper stage in the human life course is buttressed by evidence from both psychology and anthropology. The lab research demarcates the onset of this stage and shows its continuation at least until thirty-six months. Ethnographic research shows continuity and change as "helping" gets transformed into working in middle childhood – the end of the helper stage. By middle childhood, children may not operate as helpers as often because they now have their own chores, perhaps assisted by a younger sibling. Accumulating ethnographic evidence from studies of WEIRD families shows that children may lose the motivation to be helpful during early childhood. This points to the likelihood that young would-be helpers' desire to be useful and to affiliate must be accommodated. The ethnographic record shows the great diversity of such accommodations, from assigning would-be helpers to suitable tasks to permitting their participation in group projects to donating appropriately sized tools for them to use, and so on. Failure to allow the child a helper role may lead to the extinction of the motive.

While the helper stage construct may seem quite plausible, questions can be raised. An immediate question is the compromise that workers must make in their own efficiency when they accommodate young helpers. Interviews with WEIRD mothers illustrate the many strategies they employ (doing household chores when their toddler is napping) to finesse their efforts to help. The child may very well find a reward for helping through affiliation and a pathway toward a place in society, but what sustains their efforts? I argue that there are two extremely important benefits that accrue to parents and children during the helper stage and later. First, unlike the lab paradigm, helping outside WEIRD society places the child in a cooperative work activity. The child learns not just to hull rice with a mortar and pestle, they learn to work collaboratively with several others who are engaged in the multi-faceted preparation of the evening meal. The claim that children are gaining a unique and extremely valuable skill in learning to collaborate is supported in numerous studies comparing village children, who are expert collaborators, and cosmopolitan or WEIRD children, who are not.

A second significant benefit to children and their kin is that through collaboration, the novices will learn most of what they will need to know of their culture – from specific skills to language, manners, and social customs. And they will learn largely through observation, imitation, practice, and subtle feedback from co-workers – identified by Bandura (1976) as "social learning." That is, experts very rarely need to provide lessons to the learner. And here, perhaps, the efficiency lost in "helping the helper to be helpful" is regained in the near-zero investment to add a valuable worker to the domestic workforce. Not only is the child enhancing their potential fitness, the assistance that the child provides also must improve the fitness of kinspeople who receive the help as well.

Future research calls for the systematic study of the helper stage in indigenous communities and more ethnographic study of the phenomenon in WEIRD society. However, one of the most prominent effects of globalization is the imposition of formal schooling, which consistently undermines the child's contributions to the family economy. Parents with at least some secondary education may adopt the WEIRD child-rearing model and spurn child helpers. It is imperative to select research sites that are relatively unacculturated and not rapidly "becoming WEIRD." Lab studies of helping need to be redesigned to more closely fit the social ecology of societies that actually value child helpers/ workers (e.g., de Haan 1999). In current lab studies, the child is helping reach another's goal, whereas, in the village, the child is part of a collective undertaking where they will likely benefit from the goal's achievement[9]. Lab studies need to allow for helping in a multidimensional task environment with multiple participants, including other children.

---

[9] I am grateful to Andrew Coppens for this suggestion (personal communication August 6, 2019).

References

Aime, Hilary, Tanya Broesch, Lara B. Aknin, and Felix Warneken (2017). Evidence for proactive and reactive helping in two- to five-year-olds from a small-scale society. *PLoS ONE* 12(11): e0187787, https://doi.org /10.1371/journal.pone

Akhtar, Nameera (2005). The robustness of learning through overhearing. *Developmental Science* 8(2): 199–209.

Alcalá, Lucia, Barbara Rogoff, and Angélica L. Frairea (2018). Sophisticated collaboration is common among Mexican-heritage US children. *PNAS*, nas .org/cgi/doi/10.1073/pnas.1805707115

Alcalá, Lucía, Barbara Rogoff, Rebeca Mejía-Arauz, Andrew D. Coppens, and Amy L. Dexter (2014). Children's initiative in contributions to family work in indigenous-heritage and cosmopolitan communities in Mexico. *Human Development* 57: 96–115.

Bakeman, Roger, Lauren B. Adamson, Melvin Konner, and Ronald G. Barr (1990). !Kung infancy: The social context of object exploration. *Child Development* 61(4): 794–809.

Bandura, Albert (1976). *Social Learning Theory.* Upper Saddle River, NJ: Prentice Hall.

Barlow, Kathleen (1985). *Learning Cultural Meanings through Social Relationships: An Ethnography of Childhood in Murik Society, Papua New Guinea.* Unpublished PhD dissertation, Department of Anthropology, University of California, San Diego.

Barnett, Homer G. (1938). The nature of the Potlatch. *American Anthropologist* 40: 349–58.

Battiste, Marie. (2002). *Indigenous Knowledge and Pedagogy in First Nations Education: A Literature Review with Recommendations.* Ottawa, ON: National Working Group on Education and the Minister of Indian Affairs Indian and Northern Affairs Canada (INAC).

Bergin, Christi A. C., David A. Bergin, and Evelyn French (1995). Preschoolers' prosocial repertoires: Parents' perspectives. *Early Childhood Research Quarterly* 10: 81–103.

Berman, Elise (2019). *Talking Like Children: Language and the Production of Age in the Marshall Islands.* New York: Oxford University Press.

Bird, Douglas W., and Rebecca B. Bird (2002). Children on the reef: Slow learning or strategic foraging? *Human Nature* 13(2): 269–97.

Bird-David, Nurit (2015). Modern biases, hunter-gathers' children: On the visibility of children in other cultures. In Güner Coskunsu, ed., *The Archaeology of Childhood: Interdisciplinary Perspectives on an Archaeological Enigma*, pp. 91–103. Albany: State University of New York Press.

Bloch, Maurice E. F. (1988). *How We Think They Think: Anthropological Approach to Cognition, Memory, and Literacy*. Boulder, CO: Westview Press.

Blurton-Jones, Nicholas G., Kristen Hawkes, and James F. O'Connell (2005). Older Hadza men and women as helpers. In Barry S. Hewlett and Michael E. Lamb, eds., *Hunter Gatherer Childhoods: Evolutionary, Developmental, and Cultural Perspectives*, pp. 214–36. New Brunswick, NJ: Aldine-Transaction.

Blurton-Jones, Nicholas G., and Melvin J. Konner (1976). !Kung knowledge of animal behavior. In Richard B. Lee and Irven DeVore, eds., *Kalahari Hunter-Gatherers: Studies of the !Kung San and Their Neighbors*, pp. 325–48. Cambridge, MA: Harvard University Press.

Blurton-Jones, Nicholas G., and Frank W. Marlowe (2002). Selection for delayed maturity: Does it take 20 years to learn to hunt and gather? *Human Nature* 13(2): 199–238.

Bock, John, and Sara E. Johnson (2004). Subsistence ecology and play among the Okavango Delta peoples of Botswana. *Human Nature* 15(1): 63–82.

Boesch, Christophe (2013). *Wild Cultures: A Comparison Between Chimpanzee and Human Cultures*. Cambridge: Cambridge University Press.

Bogin, Barry (2006). Modern human life history: The evolution of human childhood and fertility. In Kristen Hawkes and Richard R. Paine, eds., *The Evolution of Human Life History*, pp. 197–230. Santa Fe, NM: SAR Press.

Borofsky, Robert (1987). *Making History: Pukapukan and Anthropological Constructions of Knowledge*. Cambridge: Cambridge University Press.

Bourdieu, Pierre (1977). *Outline of a Theory of Practice*. Cambridge: Cambridge University Press.

Bowes, Jennifer M., and Jacqueline J. Goodnow (1996). Work for home, school, or labor force: The nature and sources of changes in understanding. *Psychology Bulletin* 119: 300–321.

Boyette, Adam H. (2013). *Social learning during middle childhood among Aka foragers and Ngandu farmers of the Central African Republic*. Unpublished PhD dissertation, Washington State University.

(2016). Children's play and the integration of social and individual learning: A cultural niche construction perspective. In Hideaki Terashima and Barry S. Hewlett, eds., *Social Learning and Innovation in Contemporary Hunter-Gatherers: Evolutionary and Ethnographic Perspectives*, pp. 159–70. Tokyo: Springer.

(2019). Autonomy, cognitive development and the socialization of cooperation in foragers: Aka children's views of sharing and caring. *Hunter
Gatherer Research* 3: 475–500.

Briggs, Jean L. (1991). Expecting the unexpected: Canadian Inuit training for
an experimental lifestyle. *Ethos*, 19: 259–87.

Britto, Pia R., Patrice L. Engle, and M. Charles Super (2013). *Handbook of
Early Childhood Development Research and Its Impact on Global Policy.*
Oxford: Oxford University Press.

Broch, Harald B. (1990). *Growing Up Agreeably: Bonerate Childhood
Observed.* Honolulu: University of Hawai'i Press.

Callaghan, Tarra, Henrike Holl, Hannes Rakoczy, Felix Warneken,
Ulf Liszkowski, Tanya Behne, and Michael Tomasello (2011). Early social
cognition in three cultural contexts. *Monographs of the Society for
Research in Child Development* 76(2): 1–142.

Caparos, Serge, Karina J. Linnell, Andrew J. Bremner, Jan W. de Fockert, and
Jules Davidoff (2013). Do local and global perceptual biases tell us anything about local and global selective attention? *Psychological Science* 24
(2): 206–12.

Cekaite, Asta (2010). Shepherding the child: Embodied directive sequences in
parent-child interactions. *Text & Talk* 30(1): 1–25.

Clegg, Jennifer, and Cristine H. Legare (2016). A cross-cultural comparison of
children's flexible use of imitation. *Developmental Psychology* 52:
1435–44.

Condon, Richard G. (1987). *Inuit Youth: Growth and Change in the Canadian
Arctic.* New Brunswick, NJ: Rutgers University Press.

Coppens, Andrew D., and Lucía Alcalá (2015). Supporting children's initiative:
Appreciating family contributions or paying children for chores. In
Maricela Correa-Chávez, Rebeca Mejía-Arauz, and Barbara Rogoff,
eds., *Children Learn by Observing and Contributing to Family and
Community Endeavors: A Cultural Paradigm*, pp. 91–112. Vol. 49 of
Advances in Child Development and Behavior. Cambridge, MA:
Academic Press.

Coppens, Andrew D., Lucía Alcalá, Barbara Rogoff, and Rebeca Mejía-Arauz
(2018). Children's contributions in family work: Two cultural paradigms.
In Tracey Skelton, Samatha Punch, and Robert M. Vanderbeck, eds.,
Families, Intergenerationality, and Peer Group Relations, pp. 2–22.
Singapore: Springer.

Correa-Chávez, Maricela (2016). Cultural patterns of collaboration and communication while working together among U.S. Mexican heritage
children. *Learning, Culture and Social Interaction* 11: 130–41.

Correa-Chávez, Maricela, Rebeca Mejía-Arauz, and Barbara Rogoff, eds. (2015). *Children Learn by Observing and Contributing to Family and Community Endeavors: A Cultural Paradigm.* Vol. 49 of *Advances in Child Development and Behavior.* Cambridge, MA: Academic Press.

Cristia, Alejandrina, Emmanuel Dupoux, Michael Gurven, and Jonathan Stieglitz (2017). Child-directed speech is infrequent in a forager-farmer population. *Child Development*, pp. 1–15. https://doi.org/10.1111/cdev.12974

Crittenden, Alyssa N. (2016a). To share or not to share? Social processes of learning to share food among Hadza hunter-gatherer children. In Hideaki Terashima and Barry S. Hewlett, eds., *Social Learning and Innovation in Contemporary Hunter-Gatherers: Evolutionary and Ethnographic Perspectives*, pp. 61–70. Tokyo: Springer.

(2016b). Children's foraging and play among the Hadza: The evolutionary significance of "Work Play." In Courtney L. Meehan and Alyssa N. Crittenden, eds., *Childhood: Origins, Evolution, and Implications*, pp. 155–72 Santa Fe, NM: School for Advanced Research Press.

Crittenden, Alyssa N., Nancy L. Conklin-Brittain, David A. Zes, Margaret J. Schoeninger, and Frank W. Marlowe (2013). Juvenile foraging among the Hadza: Implications for human life history. *Evolution and Human Behavior* 34: 299–304.

Crittenden Alyssa N., and David A. Zes (2015). Food sharing among Hadza hunter-gatherer children. *PLoS ONE* 10(7): e0131996. doi:10.1371/

Dahl, Audun (2015). The developing social context of infant helping in two U.S. samples. *Child Development* 86: 1080–93, doi:10.1111/cdev.1236.

Dahl, Audun, Emma Satlof-Bedrick, Stuart I. Hammond, Jesse K. Drummond, Whitney E. Waugh, and Celia Brownell (2017). Explicit scaffolding increases simple helping in younger infants. *Developmental Psychology* 53: 407–16.

Damas, David (2011). The Copper Eskimo. In Marco G. Bicchieri, ed., *Hunters and Gatherers Today: A Socioeconomic Study of Eleven Such Cultures in the Twentieth Century*, pp. 3–50. New York: Holt, Rinehart and Winston, Inc.

Davis, Helen E. and Elizabeth Cashdan (2020). You don't have to know where your kids are, just where they aren't: exploring free-range parenting in the Bolivian Amazon. In Brien K. Ashdown and Amanda Faherty, eds., *Parents and Caregivers Across Cultures: Positive Development from Infancy Through Adulthood.* New York: Springer

de Haan, Mariëtte (2001). Intersubjectivity in models of learning and teaching: Reflection from a study of teaching and learning in a Mexican Mazahua community. In Seth Chaiklin, ed., *The Theory and Practice of Cultural–*

Historical Psychology, pp. 174–99. Aarhus, Denmark: Aarhus University Press.

(1999). *Learning as a Cultural Practice: How Children Learn in a Mexican Mazahua Community*. Amsterdam, The Netherlands: Thela Thesis

(2018). Can we de-pedagogicize society? Between "native" learning and pedagogy in complex societies. In Julian Sefton-Green & Ola Erstad, eds., *Learning Beyond the School. International Perspectives on the Schooled Society* (pp. 28–44). Abington, Oxon: Routledge.

de León, Lourdes (2011). Language socialization and multiparty participation frameworks. In Alessandro Duranti, Elinor Ochs, and Bambi B. Schieffelin, eds., *The Handbook of Language Socialization*, pp. 81–111. Oxford: Blackwell.

DeSilver, Drew (2019). In the U.S., teen summer jobs aren't what they used to be. Pew Research Center, June 27.

de Waal, Frans (2001). *The Ape and the Sushi Master*. New York: Basic Books.

Doepke, Matthias and Fabrizio Zilibotti (2019). *Love, Money and Parenting*. Princeton: Princeton University Press.

Draper, Patricia (1975). !Kung women: Contrasts in sexual egalitarianism in foraging and sedentary contexts. In Rayna R. Reiter, ed., *Toward an Anthropology of Women*, pp. 77–109. New York: Monthly Review Press.

(1976). Social and economic constraints on child life among the !Kung. In Richard B. Lee and Irven DeVore, eds., *Kalahari Hunter-Gatherers: Studies of the !Kung San and Their Neighbors*, pp. 199–217. Cambridge, MA: Harvard University Press.

Du Bois, Cora A. (1941). Attitudes toward food and hunger in Alor. In Leslie Spier, A. Irving Hallowell, and Stanley S. Newman, eds., *Language, Culture, and Personality*, pp. 272–81. Menasha, WI: Sapir Memorial Publication Fund.

Dyson, Jane (2014). *Working Childhoods: Youth, Agency and the Environment in India*. Cambridge: Cambridge University Press.

Edel, May M. (1996). *The Chiga of Uganda*, 2nd ed. New Brunswick, NJ: Transaction Publishers.

Einarsdóttir, Jónína (2004). *Tired of Weeping: Mother Love, Child Death, and Poverty in Guinea–Bissau*. Madison: University of Wisconsin Press.

Endicott, Kirk M., and Karen L. Endicott (2008). *The Headman Was a Woman: The Gender Egalitarian Batek of Malaysia*. Long Grove, IL: Waveland Press, Inc.

Engelmann, Jan M., Lou M. Haux, and Esther Herrmann (2019). Helping in young children and chimpanzees shows partiality towards friends. *Evolution and Human Behavior* 40: 292–300.

Erasmus, Charles J. (1955). Work patterns in a Mayo village. *American Anthropologist*, n.s., 57: 322–33.

Evans-Pritchard, Edward E. (1956). *Nuer Religion*. Oxford: Clarendon Press.

Fass, Paula S. (2016). *The End of American Childhood: A History of Parenting from Life on the Frontier to the Managed Child*. Princeton: Princeton University Press.

Fasulo, Alessandra, Heather Loyd, and Vincenzo Padiglione (2007). Children's socialization into cleaning practices: A cross-cultural perspective. *Discourse and Society* 18: 11–33.

Fehr, Ernst, Helen Bernhard, and Bettina Rockenbach (2008). Egalitarianism in young children. *Nature* 454: 1079–84.

Fernández, David L. (2015).Children's everyday learning by assuming responsibility for others: Indigenous practices as a cultural heritage across generations. In Maricela Correa-Chávez, Rebeca Mejía-Arauz, and Barbara Rogoff, eds., *Children Learn by Observing and Contributing to Family and Community Endeavors: A Cultural Paradigm*. Vol. 49 of *Advances in Child Development and Behavior*. Cambridge, MA: Academic Press, pp. 53–89.

Field, Margaret J. (1970). *Search for Security: An Ethno–Psychiatric Study of Rural Ghana*. New York: W. W. Norton.

Finn, Lauren, and Maureen Vandermaas-Peeler (2013). Young children's engagement and learning opportunities in a cooking activity with parents and older siblings. *Early Childhood Research and Practice* 15(1), http://ecrp.uiuc.edu/v15n1/finn.html

Flores, Rubén, Luis Urrieta Jr., Marie-Noëlle Chamoux, David L. Fernández, and Angélica López (2015). Using history to analyze the *Learning by Observing and Pitching In* practices of contemporary Mesoamerican societies. In Maricela Correa-Chávez, Rebeca Mejía-Arauz, and Barbara Rogoff, eds., *Children Learn by Observing and Contributing to Family and Community Endeavors: A Cultural Paradigm*. Vol. 49 *of Advances in Child Development and Behavior*. Cambridge, MA: Academic Press, pp. 315–40.

Forman-Brunell, Miriam (2009). *Babysitter: An American History*. New York: New York University Press.

Fortes, Meyer (1970/1938). Social and psychological aspects of education in Taleland. In John Middleton, ed., *From Child to Adult: Studies in the Anthropology of Education*, pp. 14–74. Garden City, NY: The Natural History Press.

Fouts, Hillary N. (2005). Families in Central Africa: A comparison of Bofi farmer and forager families. In Jaipaul L. Roopnarine, ed., *Families in Global Perspective*, pp. 347–63. Boston, MA: Pearson.

Fouts, Hillary N., Carin L. Neitzel, and Lauren R. Bader (2016). Work-themed play among young children in foraging and farming communities in Central Africa. *Behaviour* 153: 663–91.

Friedl, Erika (1997). *Children of Deh Koh: Young Life in an Iranian Village.* Syracuse, NY: Syracuse University Press.

Gallimore, Ronald, Joan W. Boggs, and Cathie Jordan (1974). *Culture, Behavior, and Education: A Study of Hawaiian-Americans*, Vol. 2. Hills, CA: Sage Publications.

Gallois, Sandrine, Romaine Duda, Barry Hewlett, and Victoria Reyes-García (2015). Children's daily activities and knowledge acquisition: A case study among the Baka from southeastern Cameroon. *Journal of Ethnobiology and Ethnomedicine* 11(1): 1–13.

Gardner, Howard (1983). *Frames of Mind: The Theory of Multiple Intelligences.* New York: Basic Books.

Gaskins, Suzanne (1999). Children's daily lives in a Mayan village. In Artin Göncü, ed., *Children's Engagement in the World*, pp. 25–61. New York: Cambridge University Press.

(2013). Pretend play as culturally constructed activity. In Marjorie Taylor, ed., *The Oxford Handbook of the Development of Imagination*, pp. 224–47. New York: Oxford University Press.

Gaskins, Suzanne, Wendy Haight, and David F. Lancy (2007). The cultural construction of play. In Artin Göncü and Suzanne Gaskins, eds., *Play and Development: Evolutionary, Sociocultural, and Functional Perspectives*, pp. 179–202. Mahwah, NJ: Erlbaum

Gaskins, Suzanne, and Ruth Paradise (2010). Learning through observation in daily life. In David F. Lancy, Suzanne Gaskins, and John Bock, eds., *The Anthropology of Learning in Childhood*, pp. 85–117. Lanham, MD: Altamira Press.

Gauvain, Mary (2001). *The Social Context of Cognitive Development.* New York: Gilford Press.

Giner Torréns, Marta, Andrew D. Coppens, and Joscha Kärtner (2019). The socialization of children's contributions at home: A comparison between indigenous-Ecuadorian and German children. Paper presented at Biennial Meeting, SRCD. Baltimore, MD, March 22.

Giner Torréns, Marta, and Joscha Kärtner (2017). The influence of socialization on early helping from a cross-cultural perspective. *Journal of Cross Cultural Psychology* 48: 353–68.

Gladwin, Thomas, and Seymour B. Sarason (1953). *Truk: Man in Paradise.* New York: Wenner–Gren Foundation.

Goldschmidt, Walter (1976). *Culture and Behavior of the Sebei*. Berkeley: University of California Press.

(2006). *The Bridge to Humanity: How Affect Hunger Trumps the Selfish Gene*. Oxford: Oxford University Press.

Goldstein, Sam, and Jack A. Naglieri, eds. (2011). *Encyclopedia of Child Behavior and Development*. Boston: Springer.

Golovnev, Ivan (2004). *Malenkaya Katerina* (Tiny Katerina), documentary film. Ekaterinburg: Ethnographic Bureau Studio. https://vimeo.com /143388752. Password: TINY

Golovnev, Ivan, and Elena Golovneva (2016). The representation of childhood in ethnographic films of Siberian indigenous peoples. *Sibirica* 15(3): 83–86.

Goodnow, Jacqueline J. (1988). Children's household work: Its nature and function. *Psychological Bulletin*, 103: 5–26.

Goodwin, Grenville, and Janice T. Goodwin (1942). *The Social Organization of the Western Apache*. Chicago: University of Chicago Press.

Grove, M. Annette, and David F. Lancy (2015). Cultural views of life phases. In James D. Wright, ed., *International Encyclopedia of Social and Behavioral Sciences*, 2nd ed., pp. 507–15. Oxford: Elsevier.

Grusec, Joan E. (1981). Socialization processes and the development of altruism. In J. Phillipe Rushton and Richard M. Sorrentino, eds., *Altruism and Helping Behavior*, pp. 65–90. Hillsdale, NJ: Erlbaum.

(1991). Socializing concern for others in the home. *Developmental Psychology* 27: 338–42.

Guemple, Lee (1979). Inuit socialization: A study of children as social actors in an Eskimo community. In Karigoudar Ishwaran, ed., *Childhood and Adolescence in Canada*, pp. 39–71. Toronto: McGraw-Hill Ryerson.

Gurven, Michael and Jeffrey Winking (2008). Collective action in action: Prosocial behavior in and out of the laboratory. *American Anthropologist* 110(2): 179–90.

Hagino, Izumi, and Taro Yamauchi (2016). High motivation and low gain: Food procurement from rainforest foraging by Baka hunter-gatherer children. In Hideaki Terashima and Barry S. Hewlett, eds., *Social Learning and Innovation in Contemporary Hunter-Gatherers: Evolutionary and Ethnographic Perspectives*, pp. 135–46. Tokyo: Springer.

Haith, Marshall M., and Janette B. Benson (2008). *Encyclopedia of Infant and Early Childhood Development*. Amsterdam: Elsevier.

Hamlin, J. Kiley, Karen Wynn, and Paul Bloom (2007). Social evaluation by pre-verbal infants. *Nature* 450: 557–59.

Hammond, Stuart I. (2014). Children's early helping in action: Early helping and moral development. *Frontiers in Psychology* 5, 1–7. doi:10.3389/fpsyg.2014.00759.

Hammond, Stuart I., and Celia A. Brownell (2018). Happily unhelpful: Infants' everyday helping and its connection to early prosocial development. *Frontiers in Psychology*, https://doi.org/10.3389/fpsyg.2018.01770

Hansen, Henny H. (1961). *The Kurdish Woman's Life: Field Research in a Muslim Society, Iraq.* Kobenhavn, Danmark: Nationalmuseet.

Harkness, Sara, Charles M. Super et al. (2010). Parental ethnotheories of children's learning. In David F. Lancy, Suzanne Gaskins, and John Bock, eds. *The Anthropology of Learning in Childhood*, pp. 65–81. Lanham, MD: Altamira Press.

Henrich, Joseph, Stephen J. Heine, and Ara Norenzayan (2010). The weirdest people in the world? *Behavioural and Brain Sciences* 33: 61–81.

Hilger, Sister M. Inez (1957). *Araucanian Child Life and Cultural Background.* Smithsonian Miscellaneous Collections, Vol. 133. Washington, DC: Smithsonian Institution.

Hill, Kim R., Robert S. Walker, Miran Bozicevic, James Eder, Thomas Headland, Barry Hewlett, A. Magdalena Hurtado, Frank Marlowe, Polly Wiessner, and Brian Wood (2011). Co-residence patterns in hunter-gatherer societies show unique human social structure. *Science* 331: 1286–89.

Hoffman, Martin L. (2000). *Empathy and Moral Development: Implications for Caring and Justice.* New York: Cambridge University Press.

Hogbin, Ian (1969). *A Guadalcanal Society: The Kaoka Speakers.* New York: Holt, Rinehart and Winston.

Hollos, Marida C., and Philip E. Leis (1989). *Becoming Nigerian in Ijo Society.* New Brunswick, NJ: Rutgers University Press.

Honigmann, Irman, and John Honigmann (1953). Child rearing patterns among the Great Whale River Eskimo. *Anthropological Papers of the University of Alaska* 2(1): 31–50.

Hopkins, Brian, Elena Geangu, and Sally Linkenauger, eds. (2017). *The Cambridge Encyclopedia of Child Development.* Cambridge: Cambridge University Press.

Horn, Pamela (1994). *Children's Work and Welfare, 1780–1890.* New York: Cambridge University Press.

House, Bailey R., Joan B. Silk, Joseph Henrich, H. Clark Barrett, Brooke A. Scelza, Adam H. Boyette, Barry S. Hewlett, Richard McElreath, and Stephen Laurence (2013). Ontogeny of prosocial behavior across diverse societies. *PNAS*, 110(36): 14586–91, https://doi.org/10.1073/pnas.1221217110

Howell, Nancy (2010). *Life Histories of the Dobe !Kung: Food, Fatness, and Well-being Over the Life Span.* Berkeley: University of California Press.

Hrdy, Sarah B. (2009). *Mothers and Others: The Evolutionary Origins of Mutual Understanding.* Cambridge, MA: Belknap Press.

(2016). Development plus social selection in the emergence of "emotionally modern" humans. In Courtney L. Meehan and Alyssa N. Crittenden, eds., *Childhood: Origins, Evolution, and Implications*, pp. 11–44. Santa Fe, NM: School for Advanced Research Press.

Ingold, Tim (2001). From the transmission of representations to the education of attention. In Harvey Whitehouse, ed., *The Debated Mind: Evolutionary Psychology versus Ethnography*, pp. 113–53. Oxford: Berg.

Jiménez-Balam, Deira, Lucía Alcalá, and Dania Salgado (2019). Maya children's medicinal plant knowledge: Initiative and agency in their learning process. *Learning, Culture and Social Interaction.* 22, www.sciencedirect.com /science/article/pii/S2210656119301709?viapercent3Dihub

Jin, Kyong-sun, and Renée Baillargeon (2017). Infants possess an abstract expectation of ingroup support. *Proceedings of the National Academy of Sciences*, 114(31): 8199–204.

Jordan, Peter D. (2014). *Technology as Human Social Tradition: Cultural Transmission among Hunter-Gatherers.* Berkeley: University of California Press.

Kaplan, Hillard S., and John A. Bock (2001). Fertility theory: The embodied capital theory of life history evolution. In Jan M. Hoem, ed., *International Encyclopedia of the Social and Behavioral Sciences*, pp. 5561–68. New York: Elsevier.

Kärtner, Joscha 2018. Beyond dichotomies-(m)others' structuring and the development of toddlers' prosocial behavior across cultures. *Current Opinion in Psychology.* 20: 6–10.

Kärtner, Joscha, Heidi Keller, and Nandita Chaudhary (2010). Cognitive and social influences on early prosocial behavior in two sociocultural contexts. *Developmental Psychology* 46: 905–14.

Katz, Cindi (1986). Children and the environment: Work, play and learning in rural Sudan. *Children's Environment Quarterly* 3(4): 43–51.

Klein, Wendy, Anthony Graesch, and Carolina Izquierdo (2009). Children and chores: A mixed-methods study of children's household work in Los Angeles families. *Anthropology of Work Review*, 30: 98–109.

Kline, Michelle A., Rubeena Shamsudheen, and Tanya Broesch (2018). Variation is the universal: Making cultural evolution work in developmental psychology.

Philosophical Transactions of the Royal Society B 373(1743): 20170059, http://dx.doi.org/10.1098/rstb.2017.0059

Konner, Melvin J. (1976). Maternal care, infant behavior and development among the !Kung. In Richard B. Lee and Irven DeVore, eds., *Studies of the !Kung San and Their Neighbors*, pp. 218–45. Cambridge, MA: Harvard University Press.

Koster, Jeremy M., Orlando Bruno, and Jessica L. Burns (2016). Wisdom of the elders? Ethnobiological knowledge across the lifespan. *Current Anthropology* 57: 113–21.

Köster, Moritz, Lilia Cavalcante, Rafael V.C. Carvalho, Briseida D. Resende, Joscha Kärtner (2016). Cultural influences on toddlers' prosocial behavior: How maternal task assignment relates to helping others. *Child Development* 87(6): 1727–38.

Kramer, Karen L. (2002). Variation in juvenile dependence: Helping behavior among Maya children. *Human Nature* 13: 299–325.

(2011). The evolution of parental care and recruitment of juvenile help. *Trends in Ecology and Evolution* 26: 533–40.

(2019). Cooperative childhood model: Child development in traditional societies. Paper presented at Society for Psychological Anthropology Biennial meeting, Santa Fe, NM, April 4.

Kramer, Karen L., and Russell D. Greaves (2011). Juvenile subsistence effort, activity levels, and growth patterns. *Human Nature* 22: 303–26.

Lancy, David F. (1996). *Playing on the Mother Ground: Cultural Routines for Children's Development*. New York: Guilford Pub.

(2012). The chore curriculum. In Gerd Spittler and Michael Bourdillion, eds., *African Children at Work: Working and Learning in Growing Up*, pp. 23–57. Berlin: Lit Verlag.

(2014). "Babies aren't persons:" A survey of Delayed Personhood. In Heidi Keller and Hiltrud Otto, eds., *Different Faces of Attachment: Cultural Variations of a Universal Human Need*, pp. 66–112. Cambridge: Cambridge University Press.

(2015a). Children as a reserve labor force. *Current Anthropology* 56: 545–68.

(2015b). *The Anthropology of Childhood: Cherubs, Chattel, Changelings*, 2nd ed. Cambridge: Cambridge University Press.

(2016a). Playing with knives: The socialization of self-initiated learners. *Child Development* 87: 654–65.

(2016b). Teaching: Natural or cultural? In Dan Berch and David Geary, eds., *Evolutionary Perspectives on Education and Child Development*, pp. 32–65. Heidelberg, DE: Springer.

(2017a). *Raising Children: Surprising Insights from Other Cultures.* Cambridge: Cambridge University Press.

(2017b). *Homo Faber Juvenalis:* A multidisciplinary survey of children as tool makers/users. *Childhood in the Past* 10: 1–19.

(2018). *Anthropological Perspectives on Children as Helpers, Workers, Artisans and Laborers.* New York: Palgrave-Macmillan.

Lancy, David F., and M. Annette Grove (2011). "Getting noticed": Middle childhood in cross-cultural perspective. *Human Nature* 22: 281–302.

Lave, Jean, and Etienne Wenger (1991). *Situated Learning: Legitimate Peripheral Participation.* Cambridge: Cambridge University Press.

Lee, Dorothy (1961). *Freedom and Culture.* New York: Prentice-Hall.

(1967). A socio-anthropological view of independent learning. In Gerald T. Gleason, ed., *The Theory and Nature of Independent Learning,* pp. 51–64. Scranton, PA: International Textbook Publishers.

Leibel, Manfred (2004). *A Will of Their Own: Cross Cultural Perspectives on Working Children.* London: ZED.

Leverette, Mary M. (2019). How to use laundry to teach kids learning skills. *The Spruce.* July 24, www.thespruce.com/how-laundry-helps-teach-kids-learning-skills-2146525

Levine, Donald N. (1965). *Wax and Gold: Tradition and Innovation in Ethiopian Culture.* Chicago: University of Chicago Press.

LeVine, Robert A. (2007). Ethnographic studies of childhood: A historical overview. *American Anthropologist* 109: 247–60.

LeVine, Robert A., and Barbara B. LeVine (1963). Nyansongo: A Gusii community in Kenya. In Beatrice Blyth Whiting, ed., *Six Cultures: Studies of Child Rearing,* pp. 15–202. New York: John Wiley and Sons, Inc.

Lew-Levy, Sheina, and Adam H. Boyette (2018). Evidence for the adaptive learning function of work and work-themed play among Aka forager and Ngandu farmer children from the Congo Basin. *Human Nature,* https://doi.org/10.17863/CAM.15690

Lew-Levy, Sheina, Alyssa N. Crittenden, Adam H. Boyette, Ibrahim A. Mabulla, Barry S. Hewlett, and Michael E. Lamb (2019). Inter- and intra-cultural variation in learning-through-participation among Hadza and BaYaka forager children and adolescents from Tanzania and the Republic of Congo. *Journal of Psychology in Africa,* 29(4): 309–18.

López, Angélica, Behnosh Najafi, Barbara Rogoff, and Rebeca Mejía-Arauz (2012). Collaboration and helping as cultural practices. In Jaan Valsiner, ed., *The Oxford Handbook of Culture and Psychology,* pp. 869–84. New York: Oxford University Press.

Lord, Jack (2011). Child labor in the Gold Coast: The economics of work, education, and the family in late–colonial African households, c. 1940–57. *Journal of the History of Childhood and Youth* 4(1): 86–115.

Lupo, Karen D., and Dave N. Schmitt (2002). Upper Paleolithic net-hunting, small prey exploitation, and women's work effort: A view from the ethnographic and ethnoarchaeological record of the Congo Basin. *Journal of Archaeological Method and Theory* 9(2): 147–79.

Lye, Tuck P. (1997). *Knowledge, forest, and hunter-gatherer movement: The Batek of Pahang, Malaysia.* Unpublished PhD dissertation, Department of Anthropology, University of Hawaii.

MacElroy, Mary H. (1917). *Work and Play in Colonial Days.* New York: The MacMillan Company.

Maretzki, Thomas W., and Hatsumi Maretzki (1963). Taira: An Okinawan village. In Beatrice B. Whiting, ed., *Six Cultures: Studies of Child Rearing*, pp. 363–539. New York: John Wiley and Sons.

Marlowe, Frank W. (2010). *The Hadza: Hunter–Gatherers of Tanzania.* Berkeley: University of California Press.

Martínez-Pérez, Margarita (2015). Adults' orientation of children – and children's initiative to pitch in – to everyday adult activities in a Tsotsil Maya community. In Maricela Correa-Chávez, Rebeca Mejía-Arauz, and Barbara Rogoff, eds., *Children Learn by Observing and Contributing to Family and Community Endeavors: A Cultural Paradigm.* Vol. 49 of *Advances in Child Development and Behavior.* Cambridge, MA: Academic Press, pp. 113–35.

Martínez-Rodríguez, Maria R. (2009). *Ethnobotanical knowledge acquisition among Tsimane' children in the Bolivian Amazon.* PhD dissertation, Department of Anthropology, University of Georgia, Athens.

Mauss, Marcel (1967). *The Gift: Forms and Functions of Exchanges in Archaic Societies.* New York: W. W. Norton.

Mayblin, Maya (2010). Learning courage: Child labour as moral practice in Northeast Brazil. *Ethnos: Journal of Anthropology* 75(1): 23–48.

Maynard, Ashley E. (2006). Fieldwork first, experiments later: The development of a research program in psychology based on ethnographic fieldwork. *Cross-Cultural Psychology Bulletin*, 40 (1–2): 10–18.

McClelland, David (1961). *The Achieving Society.* Princeton: Van Nostrand Co.

Mead, Margaret (1928). Samoan children at work and play. *Natural History* 28: 626–36.

   (1967). An investigation of the thought of primitive children, with special reference to animism. In Robert Hunt, ed., *Personalities and Cultures:*

Readings in Psychological Anthropology, pp. 213–37. Garden City, NY: The Natural History Press.

Medaets, Chantal V. (2011). "*Tu garante ?*" Reflections on the Transmission Practices and Learning in the Lower Tapajós, Brazilian Amazon. Paper presented at 34th Annual Meeting of ANPEd (Brazilian Educational Research and Post-Graduate Association) October.

(2016). Despite adults: Learning experiences on the Tapajós River banks. *Ethos* 44: 248–68.

Mejía-Arauz, Rebeca, Barbara Rogoff, Amy Dexter, and Behnosh Jajafi (2007). Cultural variation in children's social organization. *Child Development* 78 (3): 1001–14.

Melis, Alicia P., and Felix Warneken (2016). The psychology of cooperation: Insights from chimpanzees and children. *Evolutionary Anthropology* 25: 297–305.

Melis, Alicia P., Felix Warneken, Keith Jensen, Anna-Clara Schneider, Josep Call, and Michael Tomasello (2011). Chimpanzees help conspecifics obtain food and non-food items. *Proceedings of the Royal Society of London B Biological Sciences*, 278: 1405–13.

Mesoudi, Alex (2011). *Cultural Evolution: How Darwinian Theory Can Explain Human Culture and Synthesize the Social Sciences*. Chicago: University of Chicago Press.

Mezzenzana, Francesca (in press). Between will and thought: Individualism and social responsiveness in Amazonian child-rearing. *American Anthropologist*.

Michelet, Aude (2016). What makes children work? The participative trajectory in domestic and pastoral chores of children in Southern Mongolia. *Ethos* 44: 223–47.

Millard, Ann V., and Margaret A. Graham (1985). Breastfeeding in two Mexican villages: Social and demographic perspectives. In Valerie Hull and Mayling Simpson, eds., *Breastfeeding, Child Health and Birth Spacing: Cross-Cultural Perspectives*, pp. 55–74. London: Croom Helm.

Miller, Peggy J., and Grace E. Cho (2018). *Self-esteem in Time and Place: How American Families Imagine, Enact, and Personalize a Cultural Ideal*. New York: Oxford University Press.

Montandon, Cleopatre (2001). The negotiation of influence: Children's experience of parental educational practices in Geneva. In Leena Alanen and Berry Mayall, eds., *Conceptualizing Child–Adult Relations*, pp. 54–69. London: Routledge.

Morelli, Gilda, Barbara Rogoff, and Cathy Angelillo (2003). Cultural variation in young children's access to work or involvement in specialized child-focused activities. *International Journal of Behavioral Development*, 27: 264–74.

Newson, John, and Elizabeth Newson (1976). *Seven Years Old in the Home Environment*. London: Allen & Unwin.

Nilsen, Ann C. E., and Randi Wærdahl (2014). Gender differences in Norwegian children's work at home. *Childhood* 22: 53–66.

Ochs, Elinor (1988). *Culture and Language Development: Language Socialization and Language Acquisition in a Samoan Village*. New York: Cambridge University Press.

Ochs, Elinor, and Carolina Izquierdo (2009). Responsibility in childhood: Three developmental trajectories. *Ethos* 37: 391–413.

Odden, Harold L. (2007). *The Acquisition of cultural knowledge of hierarchy by Samoan children*. Unpublished PhD dissertation, Department of Anthropology, Emory University.

O'Kane, Caitlin (2018). "Adulting" classes teach millennials basic skills like sewing, cooking and how to deal with relationships. *CBS News*, December 14.

Orellana, Marjorie F. (2001). The work kids do: Mexican and Central American immigrant children's contributions to households and schools in California. *Harvard Educational Review* 71: 366–89.

Paradise, Ruth M. (1987). *Learning through social interaction: The experience and development of the Mazahua self in the context of the market*. Unpublished PhD dissertation, Department of Anthropology, University of Pennsylvania.

Paradise, Ruth, and Mariëtte de Haan (2009). Responsibility and reciprocity: Social organization of Mazahua learning practices. *Anthropology and Education Quarterly* 40(2): 187–204.

Paradise, Ruth, and Barbara Rogoff (2009). Side by side: Learning by observing and pitching in. *Ethos* 37: 102–38.

Paulus, Markus (2014). The emergence of prosocial behavior: Why do infants and toddlers help, comfort, and share? *Child Development Perspectives* 8(2): 77–81.

Peluso, Daniela (2015). Children's instrumentality and agency in Amazonia. *Tipití: Journal of the Society for the Anthropology of Lowland South America* 13(1): 44–62.

Pettygrove, Dana M., Stuart I. Hammond, Erin L. Karahuta, Whitney E. Waugh, and Celia A. Brownell (2013). From cleaning up to helping out: Parental socialization and children's early prosocial behavior. *Infant Behavior and Development* 36: 843–46

Phillips, Susan U. (1983). *Invisible Culture: Communication in Classroom and Community on the Warm Springs Indian Reservation*. White Plains, NY: Longman.

Polak, Barbara (2003). Little peasants: On the importance of reliability in child labour. In Hèléne d'Almeida–Topor, Monique Lakroum, and Gerd Spittler, eds., *Le travail en Afrique noire: Reprál'ésentations et pratiques époque contemporaine*, pp. 125–36. Paris: Karthala.

(2012). Peasants in the making: Bamana children at work. In Gerd Spittler and Michael Bourdillon, eds., *African Children at Work: Working and Learning in Growing Up*, pp. 87–112. Berlin: LitVerlag.

Power, Thomas G. (2000). *Play and Exploration in Children and Animals*. Mahwah, NJ: Erlbaum.

Prothro, Edwin T. (1961). *Child Rearing in the Lebanon*. Cambridge, MA: Harvard University Press.

Puri, Rajindra K. (2005). *Deadly Dances in the Bornean Rainforest: Hunting Knowledge of the Punan Benalui*. Leiden, Netherlands: KITLV Press.

Quinlan, Marsha B., Robert J. Quinlan, Sarah K. Council, and Jennifer W. Roulette (2016). Children's acquisition of ethnobotanical knowledge in a Caribbean horticultural village. *Journal of Ethnobiology* 36(2): 433–56.

Rai, Tage S., and Alan Fiske (2010). ODD (observation- and description-deprived) psychological research. *Behavioral and Brain Sciences*, 33: 106–7.

Rao, Aparna (1998). *Autonomy: Life Cycle, Gender, and Status among Himalayan Pastoralists*. Oxford: Berghahn Books.

Raum, Otto F. (1940). *Chaga Childhood*. Oxford: Oxford University Press.

Read, Margaret (1960). *Children of Their Fathers: Growing Up among the Ngoni of Nyasaland*. New Haven: Yale University Press.

Remorini, Carolina (2016). Children's skills, expectations and challenges facing changing environments: An ethnographic study in Mbya Guarani communities (Argentina). In Jessica Morton, ed., *Indigenous Peoples: Perspectives, Cultural Roles and Health Care Disparities*, pp. 31–70. Hauppage, NY: Nova Science Publishers, Inc.

Reyes-García, Victoria, James Broesch, Laura Calvet-Mir, Nuria Fuentes-Paláez, Thomas W. McDade, Parsa Sorush, Susan Tanner, Tomás Huanca, William R. Leonard, Maria R. Martínez-Rodríguez, and TAPS Bolivian Study Team (2009). Cultural transmission of ethnobotanical knowledge and skills: An empirical analysis from an Amerindian society. *Evolution and Human Behavior* 30: 274–85.

Rheingold, Harriet (1982). Little children's participation in the work of adults: A nascent prosocial behavior. *Child Development* 53: 114–25.

Ritchie, Jane (1957). Childhood in Rakau. *Publications in Psychology*, No. 10. Wellington, New Zealand: Victoria University, Department of Psychology.

Rival, Laura M. (2000). Formal schooling and the production of modern citizens in the Ecuadorian Amazon. In Bradley A.U. Levinson, ed.,

Schooling the Symbolic Animal: Social and Cultural Dimensions of Education, pp. 108–22. Lanham, MD: Rowman & Littlefield.

(2002). *Treking through History: The Hauorani of Amazonian Ecuador.* New York: Columbia University Press.

Rochat, Phillipe (2009). *Others in Mind: Social Origins of Self-Consciousness.* Cambridge: Cambridge University Press.

Rogoff, Barbara (2003). *The Cultural Nature of Human Development.* New York: Oxford University Press.

Rogoff, Barbara, Andrew D. Coppens, Lucía Alcalá, Itzel Aceves-Azuara, Omar Ruvalcaba, Angélica López, and Andrew Dayton (2017). Noticing learners' strengths through cultural research. *Perspectives on Psychological Science* 12(5), 876–88.

Rogoff, Barbara, Maricela Correa-Chávez, and Marta N. Cotuc (2005). A cultural/historical view of schooling in human development. In David B. Pillemer and Sheldon H. White, eds., *Developmental Psychology and Social Change: Research, History, and Policy*, pp. 225–63. Cambridge: Cambridge University Press.

Rogoff, Barbara, Martha J. Sellers, Sergio Pirotta, Nathan Fox and Sheldon H. White (1975). Age of assignment of roles and responsibilities to children. *Human Development* 18: 353–69.

Rohner, Ronald P. (1986). *The Warmth Dimension: Foundations of Parental Acceptance-Rejection Theory.* Beverly Hills: Sage Publications, Inc.

Romney, A. Kimball, and Romaine Romney (1963). The Mixtecans of Juxtlahuaca, Mexico. In Beatrice Blyth Whiting, ed., *Six Cultures: Studies of Child Rearing*, pp. 541–691. New York: John Wiley and Sons, Inc.

Rubenstein, Donald H. (1979). *An Ethnography of Micronesian Childhood: Context of Socialization on Fais Island.* Unpublished PhD dissertation, Department of Anthropology, Stanford University.

Schmidt, Marco F. H., Hannes Rakoczy, and Michael Tomasello (2011). Young children attribute normativity to novel actions without pedagogy or normative language. *Developmental Science* 14: 530–39.

Shostak, Marjorie (1981). *Nisa: The Life and Words of a !Kung Woman.* New York: Vintage Books.

Shweder, Richard A., Thomas R. Bidell, Anne C. Dailey, Suzanne D. Dixon, Peggy J. Miller, and John Modell, eds. (2009). *The Child: An Encyclopedic Companion.* Chicago: University of Chicago Press.

Silva, Katie G., Maricela Correa-Chavéz, and Barbara Rogoff (2011). Mexican–heritage children's attention and learning from interactions directed at others. *Child Development* 81: 898–912.

Silva, Katie G., Priya M. Shimpi, and Barbara Rogoff (2015). Young children's attention to what's going on: Cultural differences. In Maricela Correa-Chávez, Rebeca Mejía-Arauz, and Barbara Rogoff, eds., *Children Learn by Observing and Contributing to Family and Community Endeavors: A Cultural Paradigm.* Vol. 49 of *Advances in Child Development and Behavior.* Cambridge, MA: Academic Press, pp. 207–27.

Skenazy, Lenore (2009). *Free–Range Kids: Giving Our Children the Freedom We Had Without Going Nuts with Worry.* Danvers, MA: Jossey–Bass.

Sonoda, Koji (2016). Constructing social learning in interaction among the Baka hunter-gatherers. In Hideaki Terashima and Barry S. Hewlett, eds., *Social Learning and Innovation in Contemporary Hunter-Gatherers: Evolutionary and Ethnographic Perspectives,* pp. 113–24. Tokyo: Springer.

Sparks, Sarah D. (2017). Children must be taught to collaborate, studies say. *Education Week,* May 16, www.edweek.org/ew/articles/2017/05/17/children-must-be-taught-to-collaborate-studies.html

Sperry, Douglas E., Linda L. Sperry, and Peggy J. Miller (2018). Reexamining the verbal environments of children from different socioeconomic backgrounds. *Child Development,* pp. 1–16, https://doi.org/10.1111/cdev.13072

Spittler, Gerd (1998). *Hirtenarbeit.* Cologne: Rüdiger Köppe.

Sprott, Julie W. (2002). *Raising Young Children in an Alaskan Iñupiaq Village: The Family, Cultural and Village Environment of Rearing.* Westport, CT: Bergin and Garvey.

Stanton, Margaret A., Elizabeth V. Lonsdorf, Anne E. Pusey, and Carson M. Murray (2017). Do juveniles help or hinder? Influence of juvenile offspring on maternal behavior and reproductive outcomes in wild chimpanzees (Pan troglodytes). *Journal of Human Evolution* 111 (Supplement C): 152–62.

Super, Charles M., and Sara Harkness (1986). The developmental niche: A conceptualization at the interface of child and culture. *International Journal of Behavioral Development* 9: 545–69.

Svetlova, Margarita, Sara R. Nichols, and Celia A. Brownell (2010). Toddlers' prosocial behavior: From instrumental to empathic to altruistic helping. *Child Development* 81: 1814–27.

Taggart, Jessica, Eren Fukuda, and Angeline Lillard (2018). Children's preference for real activities: Even stronger in the Montessori Children's House. *Journal of Montessori Research* 4(2): 1–9.

Taggart, Jessica, Megan J. Heise, and Angeline S. Lillard (2017). The real thing: Preschoolers prefer actual activities. *Developmental Science* 21(3), https://doi.org/10.1111/desc.12852

Tomasello, Michael (2009). *Why We Cooperate.* Cambridge, MA: MIT Press.

Tomasello, Michael, and Amrisha Vaish (2013). Origins of human cooperation and morality. *Annual Review of Psychology* 64: 231–55.

Toren, Christina (1990). *Making Sense of Hierarchy: Cognition as Social Process in Fiji*. Houndsmills, UK: Palgrave–Macmillan.

Trivers, Robert L. (1974). Parent-offspring conflict. *American Zoology* 14: 249–64.

Tronick, Edward Z., Gilda Morelli, and Paula K. Ivey (1992). The Efe forager infant and toddler's pattern of social relationships: Multiple and simultaneous. *Developmental Psychology* 28(4): 568–77.

Tucker, Bram, and Alyson G. Young (2005). Growing up Mikea: Children's time allocation and tuber foraging in southwestern Madagascar. In Barry S. Hewlett and Michael E. Lamb, eds., *Hunter-Gatherer Childhoods: Evolutionary, Developmental, and Cultural Perspectives*, pp. 147–71. New Brunswick, NJ: Aldine/Transaction Publishers.

Tudge, Jonathan (2008). *The Everyday Lives of Young Children: Culture, Class, and Child Rearing in Diverse Societies*. Cambridge: Cambridge University Press.

Turnbull, Colin M. (1965). *The Mbuti Pygmies: An Ethnographic Survey*. New York: American Museum of Natural History.

Veile, Amanda, and Karen Kramer (2018). Infant allocare in traditional societies. *Physiology & Behavior*, https://doi.org/10.1016/j.physbeh.2018.02.054

Vermonden, Daniel (2009). Reproduction and development of expertise within communities of practice: A case study of fishing activities in South Buton. In Serena Heckler, ed., *Landscape, Process, and Power: Re–evaluating Traditional Environmental Knowledge*, pp. 205–29. Oxford: Berghahn Books.

Voget, Fred W. (1975). *A History of Ethnology*. New York: Holt, Rinehart and Winston.

Warneken, Felix (2013). Young children proactively remedy unnoticed accidents. *Cognition* 126: 101–8.

    (2015a). Are social norms and reciprocity necessary for early helping? *Proceedings of the National Academy of Sciences* 112(10): E1052–E1052.

    (2015b). Precocious prosociality: Why do young children help? *Child Development Perspectives* 9(1): 1–6.

Warneken, Felix, and Michael Tomasello (2006). Altruistic helping in human infants and young chimpanzees. *Science* 311(5765): 1301–3.

    (2007). Helping and cooperation at 14 months of age. *Infancy* 11: 271–94.

    (2009). The roots of human altruism. *British Journal of Psychology* 100: 455–71.

(2013). Parental presence and encouragement do not influence helping in young children. *Infancy* 18: 345–68.

Watson-Gegeo, Karen A., and David W. Gegeo (2001). "That's what children do": Perspectives on work and play in Kwara'ae. Paper presented at annual meeting, Association for the Study of Play, San Diego, CA, February.

Watson-Jones, Rachael E., Christine H. Legare, Harvey Whitehouse, and Jennifer M. Clegg (2014). Task-specific effects of ostracism on imitative fidelity in early childhood. *Evolution and Human Behavior* 35: 204–10.

Weisner, Thomas S. (1989). Cultural and universal aspects of social support for children: Evidence from the Abaluyia of Kenya. In Deborah Belle, ed., Children's Social Networks and Social Supports, pp. 70–90. New York: John Wiley.

Weisner, Thomas S., and Ronald Gallimore (1977). My brother's keeper: Child and sibling caretaking. *Current Anthropology* 18: 169–90.

Weiss, Florence (1993). Von der schwierigkeit, über kinder zu forshen. Die Iatmul in Papue Neuginea, in Marie-Jose van de Loo, and Margaret Reinhart, eds. *Kinder: Ethnologische forschungen in fünf Kontinenten*, pp. 96–153. München, Germany: Trickster Verlag.

Wenger, Martha (1989). Work, play and social relationships among children in a Giriama community. In Deborah Belle, ed., *Children's Social Networks and Social Supports*, pp. 91–115. New York: John Wiley.

Whiting, John W. M. (1941). *Becoming a Kwoma*. New Haven, CT: Yale University Press.

Whittemore, Robert D. (1989). *Child Caregiving and Socialization to the Mandinka Way: Toward an Ethnography of Childhood*. Unpublished PhD dissertation, Department of Anthropology, UCLA, Los Angeles, CA.

Wilbert, Johannes (1976). To become a maker of canoes: An essay in Warao enculturation. In Johannes Wilbert, ed., *Enculturation in Latin America* pp. 303–58. Los Angeles: UCLA Latin American Center Publications.

Williams, Thomas R. (1969). *A Borneo Childhood: Enculturation in Dusun Society*. New York: Holt, Reinhart and Winston.

Wylie, Laurence (1957). *Village in the Vaucluse*. New York: Harper and Row.

Wynn, Karen (2009). Constraints on natural altruism. *British Journal of Psychology* 100: 481–85.

Zeiher, Helga (2001). Dependent, independent, and interdependent relations: Children as members of the family household in West Berlin. In Leena Alanen and Berry Mayall, eds., *Conceptualizing Child–Adult Relations*, pp. 37–53. London: Routledge.

Zempleni-Rabain, Jacqueline (1973). Food and strategy involved in learning fraternal exchange among Wolof children. In Pierre Alexandre, ed.,

French Perspective in African Studies, pp. 220–33. London: Oxford University Press for the International African Institute.

Zepeda, Lydia, and Jongsoog Kim (2006). Farm parents' views on their children's labour on family farms: A focus group study of Wisconsin dairy farmers. *Agriculture and Human Values* 23: 109–21.

Acknowledgments

I am grateful to Alyssa Crittenden and the Society for Cross-Cultural Research for inviting me to present an early version of these ideas at the 2018 conference in Las Vegas. I owe an enormous debt to eHRAF, the electronic Human Relations Area Files, headquartered at Yale, and to the Merrill-Cazier Library and staff at Utah State University. As always, I cite the invaluable editorial assistance of Jennifer J. Green Delliskave.

For Adley, with the wish she grows up to be helpful and generous.

Cambridge Elements ≡

Psychology and Culture

Kenneth D. Keith

University of San Diego

Kenneth D. Keith is author or editor of more than 160 publications on cross-cultural psychology, quality of life, intellectual disability, and the teaching of psychology. He was the 2017 president of the Society for the Teaching of Psychology.

About the Series

Elements in Psychology and Culture features authoritative surveys and updates on key topics in cultural, cross-cultural, and indigenous psychology. Authors are internationally recognized scholars whose work is at the forefront of their subdisciplines within the realm of psychology and culture.

Cambridge Elements ≡

Psychology and Culture

Elements in the Series

A full series listing is available at: www.cambridge.org/EPAC

Printed in the United States
By Bookmasters